First World War
and Army of Occupation
War Diary
France, Belgium and Germany

19 DIVISION
Divisional Troops
Divisional Signal Company
16 July 1915 - 31 October 1918

WO95/2070/2

The Naval & Military Press Ltd
www.nmarchive.com
Published in association with The National Archives

Published by

The Naval & Military Press Ltd

Unit 10 Ridgewood Industrial Park,

Uckfield, East Sussex,

TN22 5QE England

Tel: +44 (0) 1825 749494

www.naval-military-press.com

www.nmarchive.com

This diary has been reprinted in facsimile from the original. Any imperfections are inevitably reproduced and the quality may fall short of modern type and cartographic standards.

© Crown Copyright
Images reproduced by permission of The National Archives, London, England, 2015.

Contents

Document type	Place/Title	Date From	Date To
Heading	WO95/2070/2		
Heading	19th Divl Signal Coy. R.E. Jly 1915-Oct 1918		
Heading	19th Division Divl: 19th Signal Coy: R.E. Vol I 16-31-7-15 Oct 18		
War Diary	Bulford	16/07/1915	16/07/1915
War Diary	Southampton	16/07/1915	16/07/1915
War Diary	Havre	17/07/1915	18/07/1915
War Diary	St Omer	20/07/1915	20/07/1915
War Diary	Tilques	23/07/1915	23/07/1915
War Diary	Ebblinghem	24/07/1915	24/07/1915
War Diary	Norrent Fontes	25/07/1915	25/07/1915
War Diary	Busnes	31/07/1915	31/07/1915
Heading	19th Division 19th Divisional Signal Coys Vol: II from 31 Jly to 31 Aug 15		
War Diary	Merville	31/07/1915	31/08/1915
Diagram etc	Appendix no 1		
Diagram etc			
Miscellaneous	A Form. Messages And Signals.		
Heading	19th Division 19th Divl Signal Coy: vol 3 Sept 15		
War Diary	Loisne	19/09/1915	29/09/1915
Heading	19th Division 19th Signal Coy: R.E. Vol 4 Oct 15		
War Diary	Locon	03/10/1915	03/10/1915
War Diary	La Fosse	14/10/1915	21/10/1915
Map	Identification Trace for use with Artillery Maps. Appendix II		
Heading	19th Div. Sig: Coy: Vol 5 Nov 15		
War Diary	Locon	20/11/1915	25/11/1915
Diagram etc	Proposed Communications 19th Division Reserve Area Appx I		
Heading	19th Inf: Sir: Coy: Vol 6 Dec 1915		
War Diary	Locon	04/12/1915	29/12/1915
Heading	19th Div. Signal Coy. Vol 6		
Map			
Heading	19th Signals. Vol 7 Jan 16		
War Diary	Lestrem	01/01/1916	24/01/1916
War Diary	St Venant	02/02/1916	24/02/1916
Diagram etc			
Heading	19 Div Signals Vol 9		
Heading	War Diary of 19th Divisional Signal Coy R.E. from 1st March 1916 to 31st March 1916 (Volume 9)		
War Diary	In The Field	05/03/1916	25/03/1916
Map	Report Centre Lines Of 19th Div. Until Completion Of Comic Airline System Appendix I		
Map			
War Diary	In The Field	02/04/1916	22/04/1916
War Diary	Norrent Fontes	07/05/1916	07/05/1916
War Diary	Flesselles	09/05/1916	15/06/1916
War Diary	St Gratien	16/06/1916	27/06/1916
War Diary	In The Fields	05/07/1916	31/07/1916

Heading	19th Divisional Engineers 19th Divisional Signals Company R.E. August 1916		
War Diary	In The Field	01/08/1916	30/10/1916
War Diary		11/11/1916	27/11/1916
War Diary		02/11/1916	25/11/1916
War Diary	In The Field	08/12/1916	25/01/1918
Heading	19 Divisional Signal Coy R.E. War Diary for January 1915		
War Diary	Field	15/02/1918	30/03/1918
Heading	19th Divisional Engineers 19th Divisional Signal Company R.E. April 1918.		
War Diary	Field	01/04/1918	30/06/1918
Diagram etc	Communications Of Inf Bdes. Appendix 3		
Diagram etc	19th Div. Signal Coy. R.E.		
Diagram etc	19 Div. Signal Coy. R.E. Communications. Appendix 1		
Diagram etc	19th Div. Signal Coy. R.E. Communications.		
War Diary		01/07/1918	31/07/1918
War Diary	Field	01/08/1918	31/10/1918

WO 95/20707/2

19TH DIVISION

19TH DIVL SIGNAL COY. R.E.

JLY 1915 - OCT 1918

19TH DIVISION

19th Division

101/6250

Div:
19th Signal Coy: R.E.
Vol: I

16-10-16-7-18

Oct 18

Army Form C. 2118

WAR DIARY
or
INTELLIGENCE SUMMARY
(Erase heading not required.)

19th Div Sig Coy R.E.

Place	Date	Hour	Summary of Events and Information	Remarks and references to Appendices
Bulford	16-7-15	10.0 am	Entrained for Southampton.	MS
Southampton	16-7-15	3.0 pm	Entrained on S.S. Invicta for Havre.	MS
Havre	17-7-15	1.0 pm	Dis-Entrained & proceeded to No 5 Rest Camp. No casualties	MS
Havre	18-7-15	10.0 pm	Entrained 1 Horse (Riding) left at Havre 18-7-15.	MS
St Omer	20-7-15	3.0 am	Detrained & proceeded to Tilques. No casualties	MS
Tilques	23-7-15	8.30 pm	Proceeded by road to Setlinghem. In billets in village. No casualties	MS
Setlinghem	24-7-15	9.0 am	Proceeded by road to Norrent Fontes. Billets in village.	MS
Norrent Fontes	25-7-15	0.4 h	Proceeded by road to Busnes. One man (Sanders) accidentally killed by steelocucles 24-7-15 S89 No 2 Section	
Busnes	31-7-15	10.4 h	Proceeded by road to Annville. Billeted in town. Nothing to record	MS

Major Cape
Comm'g 19th Signal Coy
R.E.

121/6607

19th Division

19th Divisional Signal Coys.

Vol: II.

From 3 July to 31 Aug. 15

WAR DIARY or INTELLIGENCE SUMMARY

Army Form C. 2118

Place	Date	Hour	Summary of Events and Information	Remarks and references to Appendices
Merville	31-7-15	6.0pm	Arrived at Merville. C.Coys. transferred to Home Estab. to take on Communication holed Thunderstorm. All lines affected.	
do	3-8-15	—		
do	14-8-15	5.9pm	Signal office having been protected by fuses, heat coils & lightning arresters escaped injury. Several instruments at Brigade Signal Offices suffered damage to coils. One length of D5 cable tied up to poles of permanent line was struck by lightning and a portion measuring approximately fifty yards was completely burnt out. Brigade Sections have now been supplied with lightning protectors.	
do	26-8-15	8.0am	One cable detachment proceeded to Locon by road to establish communication for artillery.	
do	30-8-15	2.0pm	Company proceeded to LOCON by road less one relief in Signal Office.	
do	31-8-15	10.0am	Signal office closed at MERVILLE and opened at LOCON.	
			Circuit diagram of connections at MERVILLE attached	Appx No 1
			Chart of daily fluctuations in traffic attached	Appx No 2

V.H.Gorell Captain,
Commanding 19th Div. Signal Coy. R.E.

Appendix No 1

Posted 16/8/15

Circuit Diagram –
16th Aug 15

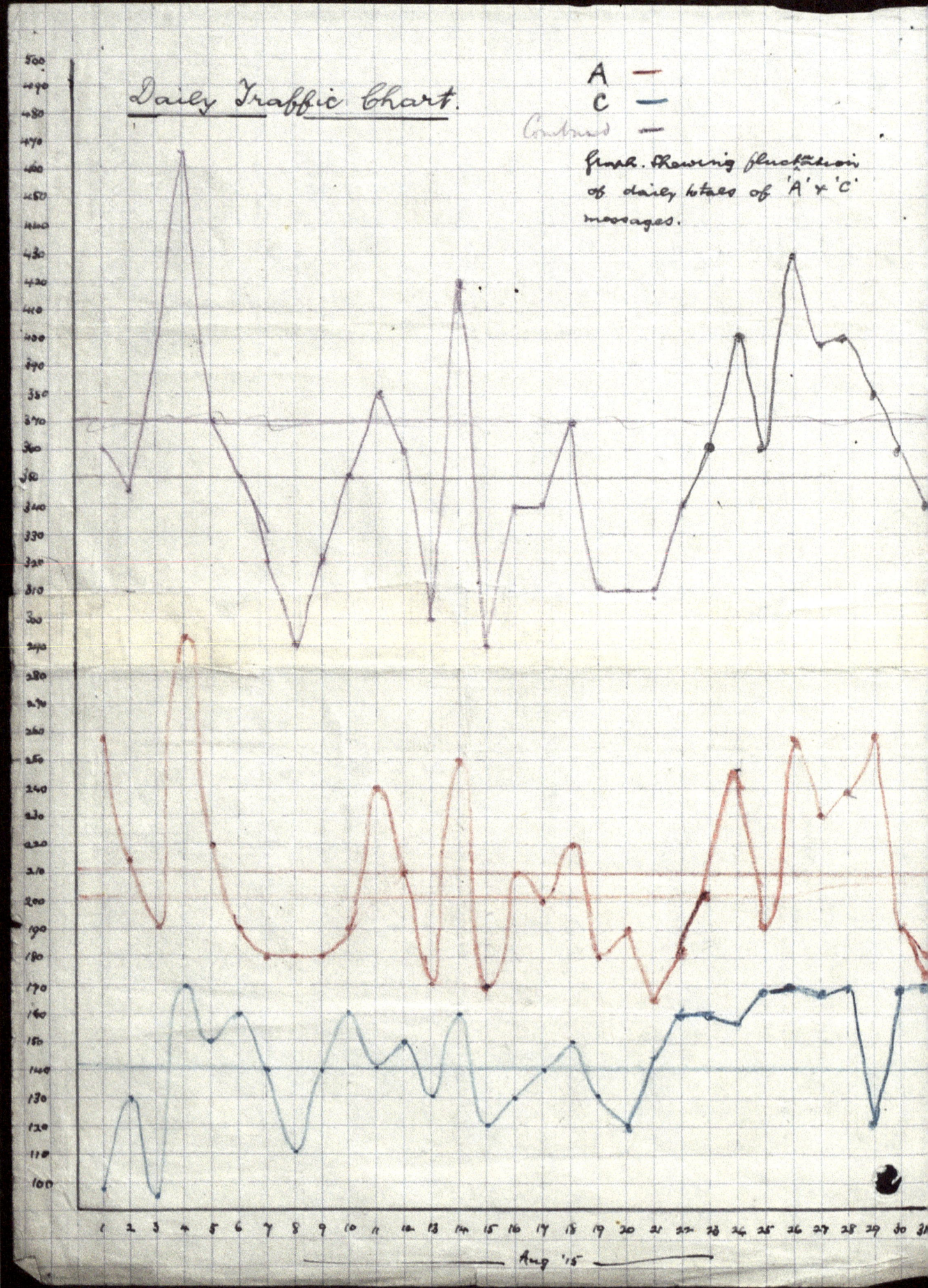

121/7153

19th Division

19th Divl: Signal Log:
Vol 3

Sep 15

WAR DIARY
or
INTELLIGENCE SUMMARY

(Erase heading not required.)

Army Form C. 2118

Place	Date	Hour	Summary of Events and Information	Remarks and references to Appendices
Locon	19/9/15		Lieut. G.I. Davison reported for duty as Supernumerary Officer.	
"	24/9/15	2.0 pm	Signal Office opened at Advanced Headquarters Report Centre (see appendix) a portion of the Company remaining at Locon to staff signal office there.	
"	24/9/15 to 25/9/16	8.30 am 5.30 am	Heavy artillery bombardment. During this period the lines to Advanced Brigade Headquarters were frequently patrolled and were undamaged except in the case of the Cavalry line to advanced 58th Bde which was wilfully cut by someone in 6 sections on 24/9/15. It was repaired before dark. Buried lines were found very unsatisfactory owing to induction. Loudspeaker lines gave excellent results.	
Loone	25/9/15	6.30 am	Attack by 58th Bde + Bdy Bde — All communications held throughout the day.	
"	28/9/15	6.0 pm	SIRHIND Bde + 1st Seaforth Highlanders joined the Divn. Communication opened with SIRHIND Bde Signal Office at 6.0 pm.	
"	29/9/15	11.0 am	Communication by telephone with SIRHIND Bde broke down. The fault was thought to be through the line running too near an electric light wire and a new line was laid in this section which gave excellent results. Rain has continued throughout the day and buried lines & lines in ditches gave poor signals.	

V. Wyatt Mayor
Comm 19th Divl Signal Coy

LOISNE
30/9/15.

121/7593

19th Division

19th Signal Coy: RE.
Vol 4
Oct 15

WAR DIARY
or
INTELLIGENCE SUMMARY

Army Form C. 2118

Place	Date	Hour	Summary of Events and Information	Remarks and references to Appendices
LOCON	3/10/15	9.30 A.M	Company moved by road to La Fosse. One relief proceeded in advance to take over Signal Office, and one relief remained at LOCON until 10 am to hand over to Meerut Divn. Office closed at LOCON 10.0 am and opened LA FOSSE same time.	Any
La Fosse	14/10/15	—	II Lieut G.S. DAVISON proceeded to England for duty with new Armies (authority, letter from A.G. GHQ No D/346 d/10/10/15.)	Any
do	21/10/15	9 am	Company returned to LOCON by road. Reliefs as before to hand over old and take over new Signal Office. Office closed at LA FOSSE 10.0 am and opened LOCON same time.	Any
			Diagram of circuits at LA FOSSE app I	
			do at LOCON app II	

[signature] Major,
Commanding 19th Div. Signal Coy. R.E.

19ᵗᵉⁿ Div: Sig: Cps:
Pol: 5

121/7624

Nov 15.

WAR DIARY
or
INTELLIGENCE SUMMARY
(Erase heading not required.)

Army Form C. 2118

Place	Date	Hour	Summary of Events and Information	Remarks and references to Appendices
LOCON	20/11/15	10.0 am	Lieut R. Juckes with one Cable detachment & 10 Office Telegraphists left Locon for St Venant to open Sub Office (Y.S.R)	
	23/11/15		58th Brigade Signals moves from Reserve Area W6D3.6 to LeSart	
	"		56th Brigade Signals moves from Loisne to Reserve Area W6D3.6.	
	24/11/15		57th Brigade Signals moves from Cse du Raux to Reserve Area W6D3.6	
	25/11/15		57th Brigade Signals moves from Reserve Area W6D3.6 to Rouceq	
			Diagram proposed Communications	Appx. I

Myrrel Major.

Commanding 19th Div. Signal Coy. R.E.

Duplicate
Appx I

Proposed Communications.

19th Division
Reserve Area.

ZEP — KOG, ELG, SLG, NLG

ZEH — CHEI, RWPI, WEI, WIP

FYS — FHF, PHG, FHH, FHI, EQHI

YSR (St Venant) — SWB, Train

LCO (Merville)

YDF (Lestrem)

CRE

ZEG — RWJ, GLH, WOT, NSH

YS (Locon)

YG

Legend:
- D3 Telephone
- Ringing Telephone
- Sounder
- Vibrator

19ᵗʰ Stnl: Sg: Coy:
vol: 6

798/12/15

Dec 1915

WAR DIARY
or
INTELLIGENCE SUMMARY
(Erase heading not required.)

Army Form C. 2118

Place	Date	Hour	Summary of Events and Information	Remarks and references to Appendices
LOCON	4/17/15	6.0pm	Lieut Snetko R.E. with one Cable section left St Venant for LOCON and the Sub office at St Venant was closes at this hour.	my
"	3/17/15	11.0am	No. 57048 C.Q.M.S. Atkins J.H. evacuates to 59th Field Amb.	my
"	"	9.10am	Advance party of office Telegraphists left LOCON for Lestrem to take over office from 46th Divisional Signal Coy R.E. The remainder of the Company leaving office as LOCON had closed. This was done at 11.0am.	my
"	3/17/15	10.0am	58th Brigade Signals moves from Le Sart to Cse du Raux	my
"	4/12/15	9am	57th " " " Robecq " Veille Chapelle spending night of 4/12/15 at LOCON	my
"	4/12/15	10am	56th " " " Les Lauriers " Les 8 Maisons	my
"	11/12/15	10.0am	58th Brigade Signals moves from Cse du Raux to Veille Chapelle.	my
"	"	"	57th " " " " Veille Chapelle " Cse du Raux	my
"	18/12/15	10.0am	58th Brigade Signals moves from Veille Chapelle to Les 8 Maisons	my
"	"	"	56th " " " Les 8 Maisons " Veille Chapelle	my
"	29/12/15	10.0am	56th Brigade Signals moves from Vieille Chapelle to Cse du Raux	my
"	"	"	57th " " " " Cse du Raux " Vielle Chapelle	my
"	29/12/15	11.4pm	Lieut Stroud R.E. joined for instruction.	Diagram showing Divisional & Arty Lines App No 1

[signature] Major
Commanding 19th Div. Signal Coy. R. E.

19th Div. Signal Coy.
Vol: 6.
Enclosures to 121/7928

A.G.7
S.D.2
D.F.W.
M.T.2
E.R.E.

19 Esjialo
2 Vol: 7
Tan'1c

Army Form C. 2118

WAR DIARY
or
INTELLIGENCE SUMMARY
(Erase heading not required.)

Instructions regarding War Diaries and Intelligence Summaries are contained in F.S. Regs., Part II. and the Staff Manual respectively. Title Pages will be prepared in manuscript.

Place	Date	Hour	Summary of Events and Information	Remarks and references to Appendices
LESTREM	1/1/16	2.0pm	Lieut Plotts M.G. R.E (S.R) joined unit as temporarily attached Officer. Lieut Littlefield	
	2/1/16	"	Lieut Mitcheson RN R.E. (T.C) left on course of instruction in trades at G.H.Q. Lieut Plotts relieving	
	5/1/16	4.0pm	Lieut Stroud F.L. R.E. (T.C) left for duty with II Corps	
	15/1/16		Major Gosset C.B. (Cheshire Regt) granted leave to United Kingdom 16/1/16 to 25/1/16 Inclusive.	
	19/1/16	2.0pm	II Lieut Howes F.N. R.E. (T.C) joined for instruction	
	26/1/16	11.0pm	do do left for duty with II Corps	
	4/1/16	12.Noon	No 4 Section 58th Inf Bde Signals moves from Les 8 Maisons R30C.6.9 to Vielle Chapelle R34 A3.6	
	14/1/16	3.0pm	do do do Vielle Chapelle R34 A3.6 to Cse du Raux X17C 7.1	
	23/1/16	3.0pm	do do do Cse du Raux X17C 7.1 to Vielle Chapelle R34 A3.6	
	25/1/16	12.0noon	do do do Vielle Chapelle R34 A3.6 to Les Lauriers K15 D10.2	
	4/1/16	midnight	No 3 Section 57th Inf Bde Signals moves from Vielle Chapelle R34a. to Les 8 Maisons R30a.	
	22/1/16	do	do do Les 8 Maisons R30a to Robecq P29.	
	7/1/16	2.0pm	No 2 Section 56th Inf Bde Signals moves from Cse du Raux X17 C7.0 to Les Lauriers K15 C0.2	
	12/1/16	10.0am	do do Les Lauriers K15 C0.2 to Calonne-Sur-la-Lys Q9.B 7.8	
	31/1/16	9.0am	do do Calonne-Sur-la-Lys Q9.B7.8 to Estree Blanche M28-29 (for purpose of Divisional Training.)	
	23/1/16	10.0am	Advance party of office Staff etc left Lestrem for St Venant ready to take over office at 9.0am on 24/1/16 from 38th Divl Signal Coy R.E.	
	24/1/16	9.0am	Company moves from Lestrem to St Venant arriving there about 12.0 noon. Office at Lestrem closed at 10.0am. Office Staff having immediately afterwards for St Venant. Office at St Venant opened at 10.0am.	Appendix II Diagram of Circuits

W. Gosset Major

Army Form C. 2118

WAR DIARY
or
INTELLIGENCE SUMMARY
(Erase heading not required.)

Instructions regarding War Diaries and Intelligence Summaries are contained in F. S. Regs., Part II. and the Staff Manual respectively. Title Pages will be prepared in manuscript.

Place	Date	Hour	Summary of Events and Information	Remarks and references to Appendices
St Venant	2-2-16	2.0 pm	Major C.B. Gosset (Cheshire Regt) O.C. 19th Div Signal Coy R.E. left for course of Wireless at Grand Quevilde. Lieut W. Ivor Bell R.E. assuming temporary Command during his absence	
	4-2-16	2.0 pm	C.Q.M.S. Atkins T.H. rejoined Unit from Signal Depot	
	7-2-16		Lieut Taylor. P. R.E. (T.C.) granted leave to United Kingdom 7/2/16 to 10/2/16 incl. rodays	
	9-2-16		Major C.A. Gosset, Cheshire Regt evacuated to M.T. General Hospital	
	10-2-16		" do died in do	
	14-2-16	9.0 am	Advance party left St Venant for La Gorgue to reconnitre + take charge of stores.	
	16-2-16	8.30 am	" of Office Telegraphists left St Venant for La Gorgue and took over Office from Guards Divn at 11.0 am	
		9.0 am	Remainder of Company moved off for La Gorgue, arriving there about 2.0 pm	
	20-2-16	3.30 pm	Lieut N.C. Platts Rept for duty with Corps	
	"	5.30 pm	2nd Lieut F.N. Howes joined Unit for duty from 11th Corps	
	19-2-16		Lieut R.J. Jackel R.E. (S.R.) granted leave to United Kingdom 19/2/16 to 29/2/16 incl. rodays	
	2-2-16	7.30 am	N°2 Section (58th Infantry Bde Signals) moved from Estree Blanche M28.B18 to Callonne-Sur-la-Lys Q9.B7-9	
	16-2-16	Noon	" " " - Callonne-Sur-la-Lys. Q9.B7-9 to Les Huit Maisons R30.C4.9	
	"	"	" " " - Roberg P4.a7.2 to La Gorgue L15a 4-5	
	19-2-16	6.10 am	" " " - La Gorgue I29.a4.5 to Laventie M9b.6.9	
	24-2-16	3.0 pm	N°3 " (57th " ") " " " to La Gorgue 35 A 3-5	
	14-2-16	11.0 am	N°4 " (58th " ") " " " to Laventie M4 C 5-3	
	16-2-16	Noon	" " (" " ") " " " to La Gorgue 35 A 3-5	
	24-2-16	2.0 pm	" " (" " ") " " " to La Gorgue 35 A 3.5	Appendix N° 1 19th Div Lines

W. Ivor Bell Lieut R.E.
Commanding 19th Divl. Signal Coy. R.E.

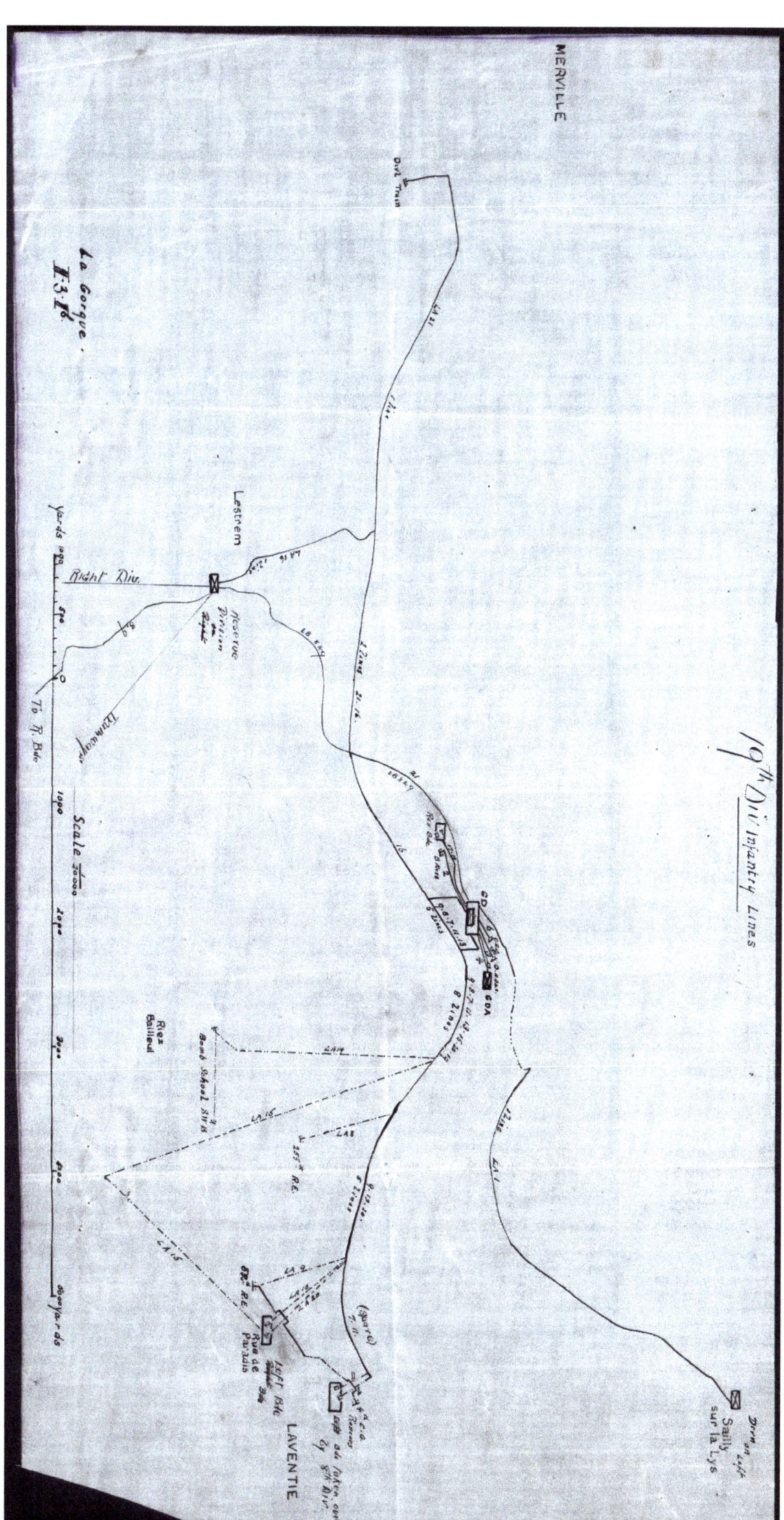

19 DW
Signals
Vol 9

Confidential

War Diary.

of

19th Divisional Signal Coy R.E.

From 1st March 1916 to 31st March 1916

(Volume 9)

WAR DIARY
or
INTELLIGENCE SUMMARY
(Erase heading not required.)

Army Form C. 2118

Instructions regarding War Diaries and Intelligence Summaries are contained in F.S. Regs., Part II. and the Staff Manual respectively. Title Pages will be prepared in manuscript.

Place	Date	Hour	Summary of Events and Information	Remarks and references to Appendices
In the Field	5/3/16	3.0pm	Major C.R. Grange R.E. arrives and assumes Command of the 19th Divisional Signal Coy R.E. vice Major C.B. Goodall Cheshire Regt (deceased)	
	10/3/16	2.0pm	Lieut P. Taylor R.E. No 4 Section (58th Inf Bde Signals) left for Signal School at Racquingham to act as Instructor vide D.D.A.S. 1st Army letter N° D.P. 960 of 3/3/16.	
	22/3/16	3.0pm	2nd Lieut H.W.I. Monk R.E. joins unit from II Corps for course of Instruction	
	29/3/16		Lieut W. Ivor Bell R.E. granted leave to United Kingdom from 29/3/16 to 4/4/16 incl.	
	13/3/16	2.0pm	No 2 Section (56th Inf Bde Signals) moved from Les Huit Maisons R30 C49 to Paradis Q24 C87	
	15/3/16	2.0pm	" " " " Paradis Q24 C87 " La Gorgue L35a44	
	23/3/16	5.30pm	" " " " La Gorgue L35a44 " Les Huit Maisons R30 C49	
	7/3/16	9.0pm	N° 3 Section (57th Inf Bde Signals) " Laventie M9679 " La Gorgue L35a44	
	15/3/16	3.0pm	" " " " La Gorgue L35a44 " Laventie M9679	
	7/3/16	5.0pm	N° 4 Section (58th Inf Bde Signals) " Cse du Raux X17C7.1 " Paradis Q24C7.8	
	13/3/16	1.0pm	" " " " Paradis Q24 C7.7 " Les Huit Maisons R29 67.8	
	23/3/16	1.0pm	" " " " Les Huit Maisons R29 67.8 " La Gorgue L35a 2.4	
	25/3/16	2.0pm	" " " " La Gorgue L35a 2.4 " Cse du Raux X17C7.1	

C.R. Grange
Major R.E.
Commanding 19th Div. Signal Coy. R.E.

— Report Centre Lines of 19th Div.
until completion of Comic airline System —

Appendix I

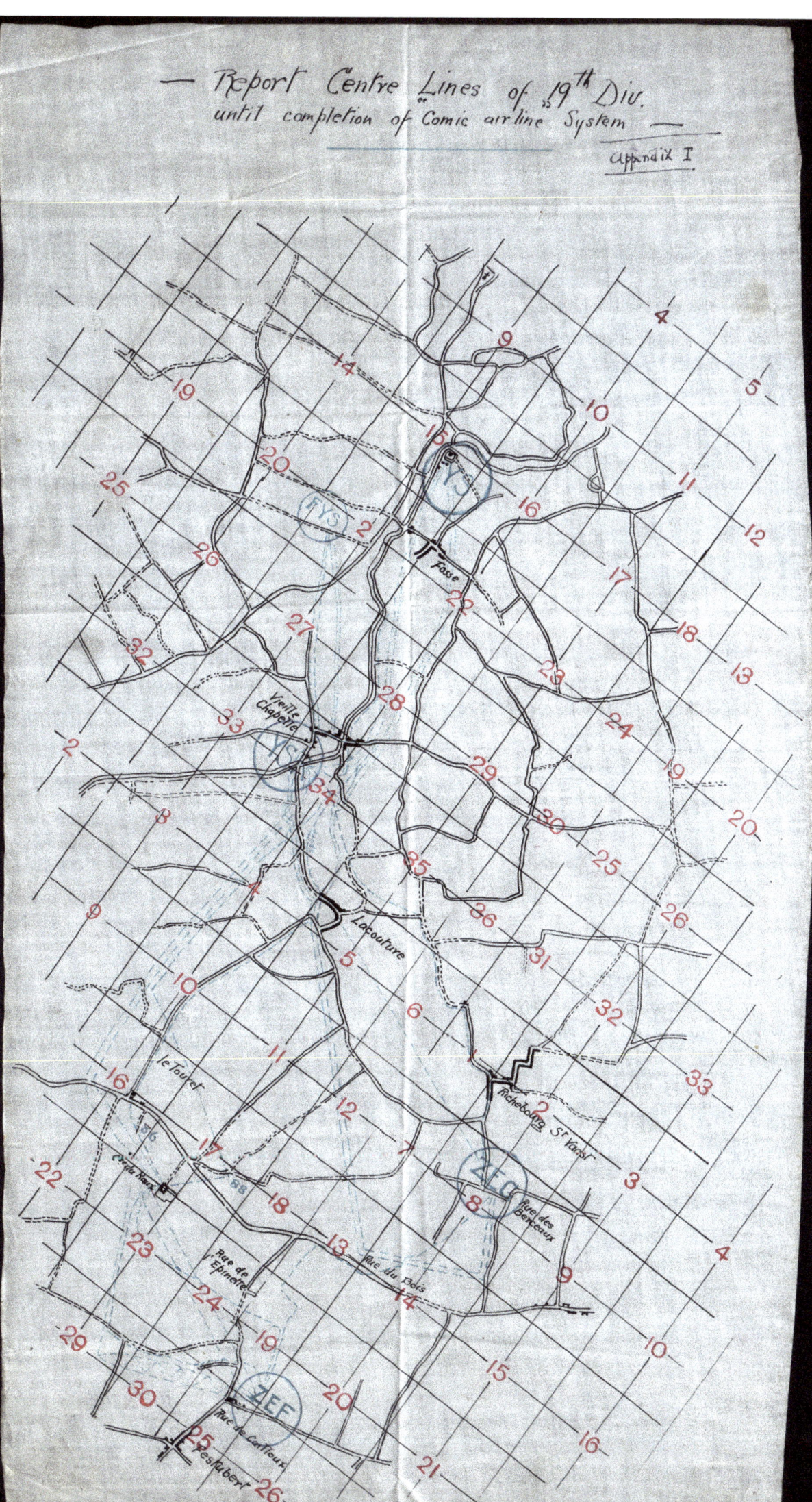

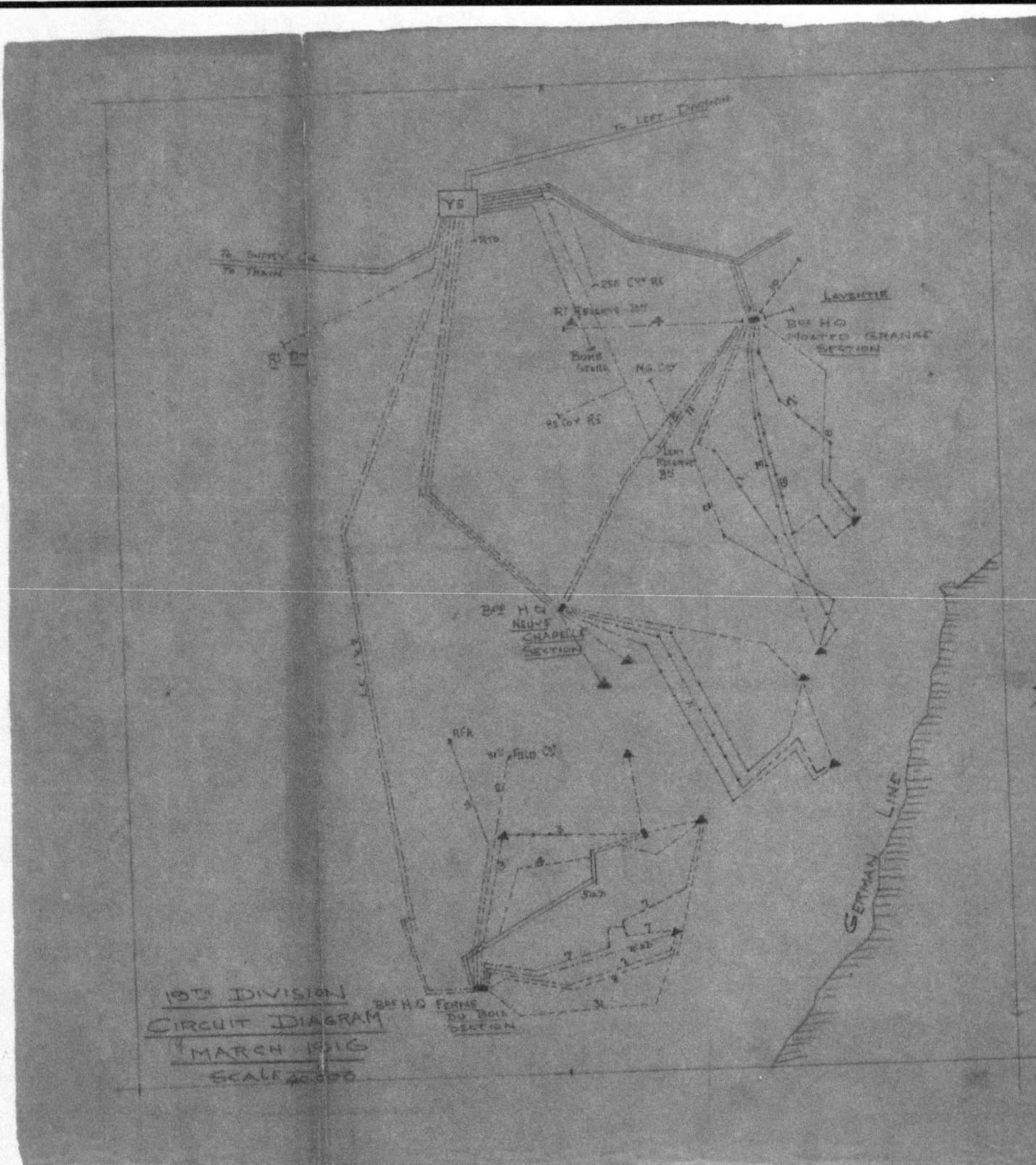

Signals
WE 192
Vol 10

WAR DIARY
or
INTELLIGENCE SUMMARY
Army Form C. 2118

Sheet No 1.

Place	Date	Hour	Summary of Events and Information	Remarks and references to Appendices
In the Field	2/4/16	1.0 pm	Lieut V.R.L. Heywood. R.E granted leave to United Kingdom 4/4/16 to 14/4/16 held to date	
	3/4/16		N° 4-9382 Sgt T.F. Wallace transferred to Home Estabt. vide D.A.G's letter N° 3239 d/d 22/3/16.	
	4/4/16	10.0 pm	II Lieut H.W.J. Monks left for United Kingdom for duty with Home Estab.	
	6/4/16	10.0 am	N° 43791 Corpl. (Motor Cyclist) G.Q. Sharp tried by F.G.C.M. and sentenced to be reduced to the ranks for being absent in United Kingdom without permission whilst on leave.	
	11/4/16		Major G.R. Grange R.E grants leave to United Kingdom from 11/4/16 to 14/4/16 held for "Investiture of Military Cross"	
	12/4/16	1.0 pm	N° 54051 Cpl. (Motor Cyclist) C. Arkle. left Unit for R.F.C. Hesdin to take up Temporary Commission in R.F.C. Auth. A.G's letter N° 1779/190ª d/d 9/4/16.	
	13/4/16	11.0 am	Lieut P. Taylor R.E left Unit for duty with XI Corps.	
	13/4/16	12.0 am	II Lieut A.J. McColgan joined Unit for Temporary duty from VIII Corps	
	15/4/16	1.0 pm	N° 54058 Corpl. (Motor Cyclist) G.T. Richardson left Unit for R.F.C. Hesdern for Probationary course prior to taking up a Temporary Commission in R.F.C. Auth. A.G's letter N° A/11997 d/d 15/4/16.	
	18/4/16	3.0 pm	Major G.R. Grange R.E evacuates "Sick" to N° 32 Casualty Clearing Stn. St Venant.	
	27/4/16	10.0 am	Major G.R. Grange. R.E rejoins Unit for duty from N°32 C.C. Stn. St Venant.	
			Changes in position.	
	17/4/16	8.0 am	Advance party left La Gorgue for St Venant to make preparations for opening offices at 10.0 am and arrived at St Venant at 9.0 am	
			Remainder of Company leaving after office had been handed over to 38th Div at 9.0 am	
	18/4/16	2.0 pm	Advance party left St Venant for Norrent Fontes to make preparations for opening offices at 9.0 am on 19/4/16	
	19/4/16	9.0 am	Remainder of Company left St Venant for Norrent Fontes arriving there about 1.0 pm.	
	16/4/16	3.0 pm	N° 2 Section (56th Inf Bde Signals) moved from Les 5 Maisons R30 C3.8 to La Gorgue L35.A3.5	
	17/4/16	Noon	" " " " to Calonne-Sur-la-Lys Q3 C9.0	
	19/4/16	8.0 am	(" " ") Calonne-Sur-la-Lys Q3 C9.0 to Rely T1 D9.8	
	26/4/16	11.0 am	(" " ") Rely T1 D9.8 to Estree Blanche M28 B0.9	

Continued.

WAR DIARY or INTELLIGENCE SUMMARY

Army Form C. 2118

Sheet No 2.

Place	Date	Hour	Summary of Events and Information	Remarks and references to Appendices
In the Field	2/4/16	5.0pm	No 3 Section (54th Inf Bde Signals) moves from Laventie (Cockshy House) M9.b.9.9t to La Gorgue L35a.4.6	
	7/4/16	5.0am	" " " " " La Gorgue L35a.4.6 to Laventie (Cockshy House) M9.b.9.9t	
	17/4/16	5.0pm	" " " " " Laventie (Cockshy House) M9.b.9.9t to La Gorgue L35a.4.6	
	18/4/16	8.0am	" " " " " La Gorgue L35a.4.6 to Robecq P2.q.a.7.2	
	20/4/16	8.0am	" " " " " Robecq P2.q.a.7.2 to Mametz g.35.6.8	
	19/4/16	10.0am	No 4 Section (58th Inf Bde Signals) " Cse du Raux x.17.c.7.1 to Vielle Chapelle R3.4.a.3.6	
	20/4/16	10.0am	" " " " " Vielle Chapelle R3.4.a.3.6 to Robecq P2.q.a.8.2	
	22/4/16	10.0am	" " " " " Robecq P2.q.a.8.2 to Erny St Julien D.35.s.s	

E. R. Lyomore Major R.E.
Commanding 19th Div. Signal Coy. R.E.

19 Div Signals
Vol 1

(Army Form C. 2118)

WAR DIARY
or
INTELLIGENCE SUMMARY

(Erase heading not required.)

Instructions regarding War Diaries and Intelligence Summaries are contained in F.S. Regs., Part II. and the Staff Manual respectively. Title Pages will be prepared in manuscript.

Place	Date	Hour	Summary of Events and Information	Remarks and references to Appendices
Norrent Fontes	7.5.16		Lieut W. Ivor Bell R.E (S.R) to be Captain from 27/4/16. Authy. III Corps No P. u.b. dd 31/5/16 & 19th Div No A/297/2 d/d 5/5/16.	
		4.30am	The whole Company moved from Norrent Fontes & marched to Berguette Station for entrainment, arriving thereabout	
		6.0am	Company entrained therefor Longreau leaving Berguette at 9.15am and arriving Longreau about 6.0pm. Officer detraining the Company marched to Flesselles via Amiens arriving about 10.30pm.	
Flesselles	9.5.16	9.0am	Lieut R. Juckes R.E. with two cable detachments left for duty with Div R. Arty at BELLOY	
	15.5.16		Lieut F.N. Howes R.E granted leave to United Kingdom 15/5/16 to 24/5/16 Incl.	
	18.5.16	9.0am	II Lieut J.M. O'Donohue 7 N. Lanc Regt ⎫ These Officers with a detachment of 8 men each joined Unit for short course	
			II " H.G. Thomas 8/Gloster ⎬ of instruction in Signalling in Trench line work prior to taking up duties	
			II " G.S. Pitts-Tucker 9/Cheshire ⎭ with Inf Bdes vide III Corps No G 257 dd 13/4/16 & 19th Div No G 4/3 dd 11/5/16	
	27.5.16		Lieut R. Juckes R.E granted leave to United Kingdom from 27/5/16 to 5/6/16 Incl.	
	27.5.16	11.0am	Two Cable detachments rejoined H.Q. from Div R. Arty at BELLOY.	
	29.5.16	6.0pm	II Lieut A.I. McGilgan R.E. (T.C) left Unit for duty with III Corps vide 19th Div No R 799 dd 26/5/16	
	30.5.16	5.0am	Sgt. Gamble with 9 men moved by Motor Lorry to St Riquier near Abbeville for the purpose of maintaining telegraphic Communications during Brigade Manoeuvres	
	31.5.16	6.0am	Capt. W. Ivor Bell R.E with one Cable detachment left for Albert to lay out new lines	
	7.5.16	8.21am	No 2 Section (56 Inf Bde Signals) moved from Estree Blanche to La Chaussee Tirancourt. (Entraining at Lillers Stn)	
	7.5.16	4.0am	No 3 " (57 " " ") " " " to Vignacourt (" " Aire ")	
	30.5.16	7.0am	" " " " " " " Mametz to Vignacourt } for Brigade Manoeuvres	
	7.5.16	3.0am	No 4 " (56 " " ") " " " to St Ricquier (" " Berguette Stn)	
	30.5.16	7.0am	" " " " " " " Erny St Julien to Flesselles } for Brigade Manoeuvres	
	29.5.16	7.0am	" " " " " " " Flesselles to Gorenflos }	
	30.5.16	7.0am	" " " " " " " Gorenflos to Drucat } for Brigade Manoeuvres	

G.R Grange
Major R.E
Commanding 19th Div. Signal Coy. R.E.

19th Div. Sigs
Army Form C. 2118
Signals
Vol 12

WAR DIARY
or
INTELLIGENCE SUMMARY
(Erase heading not required.)

Instructions regarding War Diaries and Intelligence Summaries are contained in F. S. Regs., Part II. and the Staff Manual respectively. Title Pages will be prepared in manuscript.

19th DIVISIONAL SIGNAL COMPANY
No. 893
Date 17/7/16
ROYAL ENGINEERS

Place	Date	Hour	Summary of Events and Information	Remarks and references to Appendices
Flesselles	3/6/16	9.0 a.m	Two Cable detachments left for Albert for duty.	
	10/6/16	6.0 a.m	Cpl Gamble with party of Telegraphists to report ready for duty from St Ricquier.	
	15/6/16	11.0 a.m	Advance party left Flesselles for St Gratien to prepare office.	
	16/6/16	9.30	Whole of Company moves from Flesselles to St Gratien arriving there about 12 o'ck. Office opened at 10 o'ck a.m.	
St Gratien	17/6/16	9.30	2 Lieut J.N.O'Donoghue WLanes unit attached Coy. detachment left St Gratien for duty at Albert.	
	19/6/16	9.0 "	No 3 Cable Detachment left St Gratien for duty at Millencourt	
	30/6/16	12.0 noon	Advance party of Telegraphists left St Gratien for Millencourt remainder of Company leaving at 2.0 pm arriving about 5.30 pm. Office opened at Millencourt at 5.0 pm.	
	30/6/16	11.0 "	Lieut R. Tucker R.E. (S.R.) awarded Military Cross.	
	2/7/16	10.0 a.m	No 3 Section (56 Shipshed Signals) moves from Franvillers to Flesselles	
	7/7/16	8.30 "	" " " " " Flesselles " Molliens-au-Bois	
	15/7/16	8.0 pm	" " " " " Molliens-au-Bois " Wood ½ mile W.S.W of Bazieux	
	20/6/16	9.30 "	" " " " " Wood ½ mile W.S.W of Bazieux to (Albert/Amiens) V26 B + B	
	22/6/16	9.30 "	" " " " " Wood ½ mile W.S.W of Bazieux to Vignacourt	
	10/6/16	7.0 a.m	" " 3 Section (57d) " St Ricquier " Vignacourt	
	16/6/16	7.30 "	" " " (") " " " Raineville.	
	30/6/16	8.0 "	" " " (") " Vignacourt " Millencourt	
	2/6/16	8.0 "	" No 4 Section (58d) " Raineville " La Chaussee	
	15/6/16	7.30 "	" " " (") " Dixcat " Frechencourt	
	27/6/16	8.0 am	" " " (") " La Chaussee " Bresle.	
			" " " (") " Frechencourt " Bresle.	

G.V. Grange Maj. R.E.
Commanding 19th Div. Signal Coy. R.E.

Army Form C.2118
July
19 Div Signals
VOL 13

WAR DIARY or INTELLIGENCE SUMMARY

(Erase heading not required.)

Instructions regarding War Diaries and Intelligence Summaries are contained in F.S. Regs., Part II. and the Staff Manual respectively. Title Pages will be prepared in manuscript.

Place	Date	Hour	Summary of Events and Information	Remarks and references to Appendices
In the field	5.7.16	6.0am	No. 57046 C.Q.M.S. Outhwaite to C.C.S. Albert with injured wrist (acc)	
	12.7.16	2.30pm	Company moved from Millencourt to Hennencourt arriving about 2.30pm	
	20.7.16	7.0am	Hennencourt to Albert. Cable Sections moving off at 7.0am. Telegraph Office opened at 11.0am by advance party of Operators. Remainder of Company leaving about 11.0am and arriving about 4.0pm.	
	21.7.16		Lieut W.A. Mitchison R.E. (56 Inf Bde Signals) wounded in action and evacuated	
	"		No. 58519 Sapper Callaway H. (do) Killed " near Mametz Wood.	
	"		56685 " Randall W. (57th do) Wounded " " "	
	"		45101 " Hammett G. (do do) " " " "	
	"		44804 " Leadley T. (do do) " " " "	
	"		13934 Pte Ball R. (att 56th do) " " " "	
	22.7.16		No. 98123 Corpl Harding H (19th Div Signal Coy) Evacuated to C.C.S. (Shell Shock)	
	"		43458 Spr Byron H. (57th Bde Signals) Wounded in action near Mametz.	
	"		44752 " Robinson F. (do do) " " " "	
	"		6797 A/Cpl Whittaker J. (1/ELancs. Att Signals) " " " "	
	23.7.16		No. 12612 Pte Walsh T. (M/R) " " " "	
	31.7.16		Lieut R. Tuckes R.E. Wounded in action and evacuated.	
	"		No. 66112 Sapper Smith F.C. Evacuated to C.C.S. (Severe Shell Shock)	
	1.7.16	7.30am	No. 2 Section (56th Inf Bde Signals) moved from Intermediate Line W22a to Usna Redoubt W22a	
	"	10.0pm	" " " Usna Redoubt W24a " Albert E9l.	
	3.7.16	3.am	" " " Albert E9l " "Dome" O.P. W24 d 88.	
	4.7.16	7.0pm	" " " "Dome" O.P. W24 d 88 " A–B. Line W24 d 27.	
	9.7.16	8.0pm	" " " A–B. Line W24 d 27 " Hennencourt V26 b 49	
	20.7.16	9.30pm	" " " Hennencourt V16 b 49 " Old German 2nd Line S13. b39.	
	24.7.16	9.0pm	" " " Old German Second Line S13 b 39 " Bois de Mametz X 24 a 99.	
	31.7.16	1.30pm	" " " Bois de Mametz X24 a 99 " Franvillers	

WAR DIARY or INTELLIGENCE SUMMARY

Army Form C. 2118

Place	Date	Hour	Summary of Events and Information	Remarks and references to Appendices
	1.7.16		No 3 Section (54th Inf Bde Signals) moved from Millencourt to Usna Redoubt	
	5.7.16		" Usna Redoubt " Albert	
	7.7.16		" Albert " Millencourt	
	19.7.16		" Millencourt " Becourt	
	20.7.16		" Becourt " Mametz Wood	
	22.7.16		" Mametz Wood " Bazentine Petit	
	23.7.16		" Bazentine le petit " Becourt	
	29.7.16		" Becourt " Bazentine le petit	
	31.7.16		" Bazentine le petit " Becourt	
	1.7.16		No 4 Section (53rd Inf Bde Signals) " Tara Redoubt to Albert	
	6.7.16		" Albert " Tara Redoubt	
	9.7.16		" Albert " Baizeaux	
	20.7.16		" Baizeaux " Becourt Wood	
	21.7.16		" Becourt Wood " Mametz Wood	
	23.7.16		" Mametz Wood " Bazentine Wood	
	29.7.16		" Bazentine Wood " Belle Vue Farm	
	30.7.16		" Belle Vue Farm " Behencourt	

C R Grant Major R.E.
Commanding 18th Div. Sig. Coy. R.E.

19th Divisional Engineers

19th DIVISIONAL SIGNAL COMPANY R. E.

AUGUST 1 9 1 6 ::::::

WAR DIARY or INTELLIGENCE SUMMARY

Army Form C. 2118

19th Divisional Signal Coy. R.E.

Place	Date	Hour	Summary of Events and Information	Remarks and references to Appendices
In the Field	1/8/16	6.0pm	Coy moved from Albert to Baizeu with the exception of No 3 + 4 Cable Detachments who remained for duty with R.A.	
	3/8/16	3.0"	" Baizeu " Poulanville and Bivouaced there for one night only. No 3 + 4 Dets following	
	4/8/16	6.0am	" Poulanville " Long sur Somme arriving there about 4.0 am	
	6/8/16	6.0pm	" Long sur Somme to Longpre Stations for entrainment to Bailleul. Train left Longpre about 9.30pm	
			and arrived Bailleul at 8.0 am on 7/8/16. After detraining, Coy marched to St Jan Chapelle	
	8/8/16	8.30am	" St Jan Chapelle to Westoutre and took over Office from 50th Div Signal Coy at 3.0pm (54th Inf Bde Signals)	
	8/8/16		2 Lieut F. Burnett joined this Unit from 50th Div Signals & was posted to No 3 Section (56th Inf Bde Sig)	
	8/8/16		" R.W. Stewart R.E joined this Unit for temporary duty from 50th Div Signal Coy.	
	9/8/16		Lieut E.H Triggs R.E " " duty from 4th Signal Coy and was posted to No 2 Section (57th Inf Bde Sigs)	
	17/8/16		2 Lieuts J.M. Donohue " " " " " 7/N Lancs Regt and 2 Lieut G.S.Pitts-Tucker 9/Cheshires left	
			" " " " Trench Cable Detachments to rejoin their Battalions for duty.	
	3/8/16		No 2 Section (56th Inf Bde Signals) moved from Franvillers to Govenflos	
	6/8/16		" " " " " Govenflos " Bivouacs 3/4 mile N.W of Locre.	
	9/8/16		" (" ") " " Bivouacs 3/4 mile N.W Locre to Kemmel.	
	1/8/16		" (54th " ") " " Beaucourt Wood to Bresle	
	3/8/16		" (" " ") " " Bresle " Vousbelles	
	6/8/16		" (" " ") " " Vousbelles " Bailleul	
	7/8/16		" (58th " ") " " Bailleul " Dranoutre	
	3/8/16	No 4	" (" " ") " " " Pont Remy	
	6/8/16		" (" " ") " " Bekencourt " Pont Remy	
				" " Brulooze M & DS-1

E.R. Grane Major R.E
Commanding 19th Div. Signal Coy. R.E.

Army Form C. 2118

vol 15

WAR DIARY
or
INTELLIGENCE SUMMARY
(Erase heading not required.)

Instructions regarding War Diaries and Intelligence Summaries are contained in F.S. Regs., Part II. and the Staff Manual respectively. Title Pages will be prepared in manuscript.

Place	Date	Hour	Summary of Events and Information	Remarks and references to Appendices
In the Field	2.9.16	3.0 pm	Headquarters Section moved from Westoutre to Mont Noir, Cable Detachments proceeding to Locre. Signal Office at Westoutre handed over to 4th Canadians at 3.0 pm opened at Mont Noir same hour.	
	5.9.16	7.30 am	Advance party of Office Telegraphists left Mont Noir for Bailleul and opened office there at 9.0 am. Headquarters Section following after closing office at Mont Noir at 9.0 am. Cable Detachments moved from Locre to Nieppe. Advanced Headquarters Signal Office opened there at 9.0 am.	
	5.9.16	2.0 pm	II Lieut R W Stewart left Unit to rejoin 50th Div Signal Coy R E	
	20.9.16	9.30 am	Advance body of Office Telegraphists left Bailleul for Merris and opened Office there at 6.0 pm. No 1 & 2 Cable Detachments left Nieppe at 9.30 am arriving Merris about 2.30 pm. Headquarters Section following after closing Offices at Nieppe and Bailleul at 6.0 pm.	
	20.9.16		Lieut E H Triggs R E No 2 Section (56th Inf Bde Signals) granted Special leave to United Kingdom 20.9.16 to 29.9.16 Incl 10 days. Lieut H King 3 Section (58th Inf Bde Signals) (all Signals) assuming Command of No 2 Section during period of Lieut Triggs leave.	
	3.9.16	6.0 pm	No 2 Section (56th Inf Bde Signals) moved from Kemmel to Brune Gaye	
	22.9.16	10.30 am	" " " " " " " Brune Gaye " Outtersteene	
	7.9.16	9.30 "	No 3 Section (57th Inf Bde Signals) " Pranoutre " Le Petit Mongyo Farm	
	11.9.16	2.30 pm	" " " " " " " Le Petit Mongyo Farm " Romarin	
	20.9.16	11.15 "	" " " " " " " Romarin " Outtersteene	
	21.9.16	10.0 am	" " " " " " " Outtersteene " Borre	
	25.9.16	9.30 "	No 4 Section (58th Inf Bde Signals) " Bulooze " Romarin	
	8.9.16	10.0 "	" " " " " " " Romarin " Pont-de-Nieppe	
	20.9.16	9.30 "	" " " " " " " Pont-de-Nieppe " Strazeele	

E. N. Crane   Major R.E.
Commander 19th Divl Signal Coy R.E.

Army Form C. 2118

Vol 16

WAR DIARY
or
INTELLIGENCE SUMMARY
(Erase heading not required.)

Instructions regarding War Diaries and Intelligence Summaries are contained in F.S. Regs., Part II. and the Staff Manual respectively. Title Pages will be prepared in manuscript.

Place	Date	Hour	Summary of Events and Information	Remarks and references to Appendices
In the Field	5.10.16	8.0am	Company moved from Merris to Bailleul for entrainment. Train left Bailleul at 12.25pm and arrived at Doullens about 5.45pm. After detrainment Coy marched to Marieux.	
	7.10.16	2.30pm	Company moved from Marieux to Authie. Office opened there at 3.0pm. Advanced Headquarters Operators moving with Cable Sections on to Sailly-au-Bois and opened Office there at about 4.0pm	
	17.10.16	1.0pm	Company moved from Authie to Rubempré and office opened at 3.0pm	
	21.10.16	9.0am	" " Rubempré to Warloy arriving about 10.0am and opened office at 10.0am.	
	23.10.16	8.30.	" " Warloy to Bouzincourt W14.b.8.9 and advanced H.Qrs with Cable Sections to Donnet's Post.	
	4.10.16		II Lieut F. Burnett granted 10days special leave to United Kingdom	
	26.10.16		II Lieut A. Rose R.E. Joined Unit for duty from Reserve Army Vide D. Sigs Circular No/R292 df. 27.10.16.	
	5.10.16	6.0am	No 2 Section (56th Inf Bde Signals) moved from Outtersteene to St Legev-les-Authie	
	7.10.16	2.0pm	" " " " St Legev-les-Authie	
	17.10.16	11.0am	" " " " Sailly-au-Bois	
	22.10.16	10.0.	" " " " Vadencourt	
	23.10.16	5.0pm	" " " " Aveluy	
	26.10.16	10.0am	" " " " Authille Wood W1205.5	
	30.10.16	3.30pm	" " " " Aveluy	
	6.10.16	5.30am	No 3 Section (57st Inf Bde Signals) " " " Donnet's Post W12.4.1.6	
	7.10.16	1.45pm	" " " " Bavre	
	17.10.16	8.40am	" " " " Savton	
	21.10.16	8.15am	" " " " St Legev	
	22.10.16	2.30pm	" " " " Warloy	
	26.10.16	5.0pm	" " " " Bouzincourt	
	30.10.16	1.15pm	" " " " X2.A.9.4	
			" " " " Donnet Camp	
			" " " " X2.A.9.4	

Army Form C. 2118

WAR DIARY
or
INTELLIGENCE SUMMARY (2)
(Erase heading not required.)

Instructions regarding War Diaries and Intelligence Summaries are contained in F. S. Regs., Part II. and the Staff Manual respectively. Title Pages will be prepared in manuscript.

Place	Date	Hour	Summary of Events and Information	Remarks and references to Appendices
In the Field	5.10.16	8.0 am	No 4 Section (58th Inf Bde Signals) moved from Strazeele to Outhie	
	7.10.16	10.0 "	" " " " " Outhie " Sailly-au-Bois	
	16.10.16	8.0 "	" " " " " Sailly-au-Bois " Vauchelles	
	17.10.16	10.0 "	" " " " " Vauchelles " Hervissart	
	21.10.16	8.30 "	" " " " " Hervissart " Bouzincourt	
	23.10.16	11.30 pm	" " " " " Bouzincourt " Donnet Camp	
	26.10.16	11.0 am	" " " " " Donnet Camp " X2A9.4	
	30.10.16	11.0 am	" " " " " X2A9.4 " Aveluy	

G.R. Grime Major R.E.
Commanding 19th Div. Signal Coy. R.E.

WAR DIARY or INTELLIGENCE SUMMARY

Army Form C. 2118

4th Div. Signal Company — Vol 17

Place	Date	Hour	Summary of Events and Information	Remarks and references to Appendices
	1/11/16		2nd Lieut F.N. Howes. R.E. granted leave to United Kingdom 11/11/16 to 21/11/16 incl. 10 days.	
	23.11.16	10.0 am	Coy moved from Bouzincourt Wintbg to Contay. No 3 & 4 Sections remaining with Div Arty for maintenance of communications. Office at Contay opened by advance party of Operators at 10.0 am.	
	24.11.16	8.0 am	Coy moved from Contay to Doullens. Office opened at 10.0 am.	
	25.11.16	8.0 "	" " Doullens to Bernaville. Office opened at 10.0 am.	
	5.11.16	8.0 "	No 2 Section (56th Inf Bde Signals) moved from Aveluy to Trenches X2a 9.5	
	8.11.16	7.0 pm	" " " " " Trenches X2a 9.5 to Donnet's Post.	
	12.11.16	6.0 "	" " " " " Donnet's Post " Trenches R26 b 3.3	
	16.11.16	5.0 "	" " " " " Trenches R26 b 3.3 " St Pierre Divion	
	21.11.16	8.0 am	" " " " " St Pierre Divion " Aveluy	
	20.11.16	8.0 "	" " " " " Aveluy " Wavloy	
	23.11.16	8.0 "	" " " " " Wavloy " Vadencourt	
	24.11.16	4.0 "	" " " " " Vadencourt " Gezaincourt	
	25.11.16	8.0 "	" " " " " Gezaincourt " Fienvillers	
	2.11.16	7.0 pm	No 3 Section (57th Inf Bde Signals) " Trenches X2a 9.5 " Donnet's Post	
	8.11.16	6.0 "	" " " " " Donnet's Post " X2a 9.5	
	11.11.16	5.0 "	" " " " " X2a 9.5 " Aveluy	
	17.11.16	4.0 "	" " " " " Aveluy " R26 b 3.3	
	19.11.16	7.0 "	" " " " " R26 b 3.3 " Wavloy Aveluy	
	21.11.16	10.0 am	" " " " " Aveluy " Wavloy	
	23.11.16	8.0 "	" " " " " Wavloy " Rubempre	
	24.11.16	10.0 "	" " " " " Rubempre " Bonnaville	
	25.11.16	9.0 "	" " " " " Bonnaville " St Ouen	
	27.11.16	8.30 "	" " " " " St Ouen " Gezaincourt	

Army Form C. 2118

WAR DIARY
or
INTELLIGENCE SUMMARY

(Erase heading not required.)

Instructions regarding War Diaries and Intelligence Summaries are contained in F.S. Regs., Part II. and the Staff Manual respectively. Title Pages will be prepared in manuscript.

Place	Date	Hour	Summary of Events and Information	Remarks and references to Appendices
	2.11.16		No 4 Section (58th Inf Bde Signals) moved from Aveluy to X2A94	
	5.11.16		" " " " " X2A94 " Aveluy	
	11.11.16		" " " " " Aveluy " X2A94	
	17.11.16		" " " " " X2A94 " Aveluy	
	19.11.16		" " " " " Aveluy " Zollern	
	20.11.16		" " " " " Zollern " Aveluy	
	23.11.16		" " " " " Aveluy " Warloy	
	24.11.16		" " " " " Warloy " Authieule	
	25.11.16		" " " " " Authieule " Mont Plaisir	

W. Twosell Capt. RE
Comd9 19th Div Signal Coy RE

19th D Signal Coy

Army Form C. 2118

WAR DIARY
or
INTELLIGENCE SUMMARY

(Erase heading not required.)

Instructions regarding War Diaries and Intelligence Summaries are contained in F. S. Regs., Part II. and the Staff Manual respectively. Title Pages will be prepared in manuscript.

Place	Date	Hour	Summary of Events and Information	Remarks and references to Appendices
In the Field	8.12.16	10.0 am	The whole of the Company moved from Bernaville to Beaumetz with the exception of Hdqrs. Section which remained behind for duty.	
			The whole of the Brigade Signal Sections moved in to Beaumetz on this date, with the exception of Officers relief who remained behind for duty as under:-	
			56th Bde Signals at Fienvillers	
			57" " " Gezaincourt	
			58" " " Mont Plaisir	
			A Signal School was opened at Beaumetz and is at its being carried on.	
			2. Officers & 40 men from Infantry Bdes are attending.	
29/12/16	6.0		No. 2 + 4 Secs (R.A. Signals) moved from Beaumetz to Outrebois.	
15/12/16			Capt W. Orr Bell R.E. granted leave to United Kingdom from 15/12/16 to 25/12/16 due 10 days	
9/12/16			Lieut D.R.L. Stevenson R.E. " " " " 9/12/16 " 19/12/16 " 10 "	
2/12/16			Major E.B. Brampe R.E. " " " " 2/12/16 " 12/12/16 " 10 "	
17/12/16			Lieut R.H. Tripp R.E. comes Fifth Army Signal School to instructional course 17/12/16.	
28/12/16			N.Kling Telegraphs act. 19 Div Signals granted leave to United Kingdom 28/12/16 to 7/1/17 but 10 days.	

E.R. Evans Major R.E.
Commanding 19th Div. Signal Coy. R.E.

WAR DIARY
or
INTELLIGENCE SUMMARY
(Erase heading not required.)

Army Form C. 2118

Place	Date	Hour	Summary of Events and Information	Remarks and references to Appendices
Authie Field	9/1/17	9.30 am	Coy moved from Bernaville and Beaumetz to Marieux. Office opened at Marieux at 10.00 am by advance party of Telegraphists.	
	10/1/17	12.30 pm	Coy moved from Marieux to Couin. Office opened at Couin at 10 am.	
	9/1/17	9.0 am	No. 2 Section (56th Inf Bde Signals) moved from Fienvillers to Beauquesne	
	10/1/17	11.0 am	" " " " " Beauquesne - Authie	
	22/1/17	11.0 pm	" " " " " Authie - Bayencourt	
	9/1/17	9.15 am	No. 3 Section (57th Inf Bde Signals) " " Gezaincourt - Authieule	
	10/1/17	12.15 pm	" " " " " Authieule - Bayencourt	
	22/1/17	2.30 pm	" " " " " Bayencourt - Courcelles	
	9/1/17	9.0 am	No. 4 Section (58th Inf Bde Signals) " " Monplaisir - Beauval	
	10/1/17	12.30 pm	" " " " " Beauval - The Dell	
	16/1/17		2/Lieut R.H. Wall 3/Som.L.I. Joined Unit for duty (Temp attd) vice Fifth Army No A/666/M35 dd 16-1-17	
	30/1/17		2/Lieut R.H. Wall 3/Som.L.I. " Fifth Army Signal School for Course	
			Lieut E.H. Triggs R.E granted leave to U.K. 3/1/17 to 13/1/17 = 10 days	
			" " " " " " 14/1/17 - 24/1/17 = " "	
			2/Lieut F. Burnett R.E " " " " " "	

E. V. Grant
Major R.E.
Commdg 19'th Div Signal Coy.

WAR DIARY
or
INTELLIGENCE SUMMARY.
(Erase heading not required.)

Army Form C. 2118.

Place	Date	Hour	Summary of Events and Information	Remarks and references to Appendices
Infield	1.2.17		2/Lieut A. Rose R.E. granted leave to U.K. 1.2.17 to 11.2.17 = 10 days	
	7.2.17		Capt W. Ivor Bell R.E. transferred from 19th Div Signal Coy to "O" Corps Signal Coy V Corps Vide Fifth Army A/66/1538 d/. 2.2.17	
	8.2.17		" H. Carty Thomas R.E. " " " " " " 19th Div Signal Coy	
	7.2.17		Lieut H. King 3/Seaforths att'd 19th Div Signal Coy "X" Sect. Transferred to Fifth Army School of Instruction Vide Fifth Army N° A/n.36 d/. 1.2.17	
	11.2.17		Major G.R. Grange R.E. joined Fifth Army Wireless School for Course & rejoined Unit on duty on 15.2.17	
	24.2.17		Lieut R.N. Howes R.E. joined N°15 Sqdn R.F.C. for 5 days Signalling Course	
	25.2.17		2/Lieut R.H. Wall 3/som L.I. att'd 19th Div Signal Coy left on Indian Office London Vide A.G. N° 22583 d/. 22.2.17 Fifth Army N° A/666/1678 d/. 22.2.17 D.A.Q.M.G. V Corps N° V.A.2/24. 2.17 1097/v N° A 7448/7. d/. 25.2.17	
	21.2.17	9.00 am	N° 2 Section (56th Inf Bde Signals) moved from Bayencourt to Bus-les-Artois	
	24.2.17	6.0 "	N° 3 " (57th " " ") " " " Couicelles " Waterloo Bridge	
	20.2.17	10.0 "	N° 4 " (58th " " ") " " " The Pell Jn Bls. Louvencourt	

E.V. Linge Major R.E.
Commanding 19th Div. Signal Coy. R.E.

WAR DIARY or INTELLIGENCE SUMMARY

Army Form C. 2118.

Place	Date	Hour	Summary of Events and Information	Remarks and references to Appendices
In the Field	5.3.17		2/Lieut Burnett F. R.E. Evacuated "Sick" to Hospital	
	7.3.17		" R.H. Wall 3/5 L.I. att 19th Div Signal Coy reported Unit for duty from U.K. vide A.G.s No 2/3588 d/. 22.2.17	
	14.3.17		Lieut F.N. Howes R.E. Evacuated "Sick" to Hospital	
	24.3.17		Lieut F.N. Howes R.E. Rejoined Unit for duty fm Hospital	
	26.3.17		V.R.L. Heywood R.E. Granted Special leave to U.K. 26/3/17 to 5/4/17 10 days.	
	4.3.17	10.0 am	Coy moved from Couin to Bus-le-Artois – Office opened there at 2.56 pm.	
	10.3.17	8.0 "	" " Bus-le-Artois " Beauval " " " 2.0 "	
	11.3.17	9.0 "	" " Beauval " Boquemaison " " " 12.0 noon	
	13.3.17	9.0 "	" " Boquemaison " Ramecourt " " " 12.0 "	
	15.3.17	9.0 "	" " Ramecourt " Pernes " " " 11.10 am	
	16.3.17	8.0 "	" " Pernes " Norren-Fontes " " " 11.0 "	
	18.3.17	8.0 "	" " Norren-Fontes " Steenbecque " " " 10.30 "	
	19.3.17	8.0 "	" " Steenbecque " Merris " " " 10.0 "	
	20.3.17	9.0 "	" " Merris " Fletre " " " 9.0 "	
	31.3.17	9.0 "	" " Fletre " Westoutre " " " 3.0 pm	
	1.3.17	9.0 "	No 2 Section (56th Inf Bde Signals) moved from Bus to Authie	
	9.3.17	9.0 "	" " " " Authie " Gezamcourt	
	10.3.17	1.0 "	" " " " Gezamcourt " Rebreuve	
	12.3.17	9.0 "	" " " " Rebreuve " Croix	
	13.3.17	8.0 "	" " " " Croix " Boyaval	
	15.3.17	8.30 "	" " " " Boyaval " Estrée Blanche	
	16.3.17	9.0 "	" " " " Estrée Blanche " Lambres	
	18.3.17	9.0 "	" " " " Lambres " Ebblinghem	
	19.3.17	9.0 "	" " " " Ebblinghem " Cocove	
	20.3.17	8.30 "		

WAR DIARY
or
INTELLIGENCE SUMMARY.

(Erase heading not required.)

Army Form C. 2118.

Instructions regarding War Diaries and Intelligence Summaries are contained in F. S. Regs., Part II. and the Staff Manual respectively. Title pages will be prepared in manuscript.

(2)

Place	Date	Hour	Summary of Events and Information	Remarks and references to Appendices
In the Field	1-3-17	11.30am	No 3 Section (51st Inf Bde Signals) moved from Courcelles to Louvencourt	
	10-3-17	8.30 "	" " " " Louvencourt " Gezaincourt	
	11-3-17	8.30 "	" " " " Gezaincourt " Bonnieres	
	13-3-17	8.30 "	" " " " Bonnieres " Croix	
	14-3-17	8.30 "	" " " " Croix " Pernes	
	16-3-17	8 "	" " " " Pernes " St Hilaire	
	17-3-17	8.30 "	" " " " St Hilaire " Thiennes	
	18-3-17	9.0 "	" " " " Thiennes " Outtersteen	
	21-3-17	8.30 "	" " " " Outtersteen " Bailleul	
	22-3-17	9.0 "	" " " " Bailleul " La Clytte	
	31-3-17	2.0pm	" " " " La Clytte " Waterloo Bge	
	3-3-17	5.0 "	No 4 Section (59th Inf Bde Signals) " Courcelles " Bus	
	4-3-17	1.0 "	" " " " Bus " Beauval	
	10-3-17	9.30am	" " " " Beauval " Occoches	
	11-3-17	9.30 "	" " " " Occoches " Nunce	
	13-3-17	8.50 "	" " " " Nunce " Bouvs	
	14-3-17	8.0 "	" " " " Bouvs " Fontaine-les-Hermans	
	16-3-17	9.40 "	" " " " Fontaine-les-Hermans " Thiennes	
	18-3-17	6.15 "	" " " " Thiennes " Strazeele	
	19-3-17	7.30 "	" " " " Strazeele " Caestre	
	20-3-17	8.40 "	" " " " Caestre " La Clytte	
	31-3-17	7.0 "		

C. R. Grange Major R.E.
Commanding 20th Divl. Signal Coy. R.E.

Army Form C. 2118.

WAR DIARY
or
INTELLIGENCE SUMMARY.
(Erase heading not required.)

Place	Date	Hour	Summary of Events and Information	Remarks and references to Appendices
In the Field	1.4.17	9.0 am	One officer with party of Linesmen left Westoutre for duty with Cable burying party at Hallebast	
	2.4.17	9.0 "	N° 2 Section moved from Goove Chateau to Arques	
	3.4.17	9.0 "	" " " " Arques " Hazebrouck	
	4.4.17	5.0 "	" " " " Hazebrouck " Scherpenberg	
	13.4.17	9.0 "	" " " " Scherpenberg " La Clytte	
	2.4.17	8.45 am	N° 3 Section (57th Inf Bde Signals) " Caistre " Hazebrouck	
	3.4.17	8.30 "	" " " " Hazebrouck " Longuenesse	
	4.4.17	11.0 am	" " " " Longuenesse " Westbecourt	
	17.4.17	8.30 "	" " " " Westbecourt " Arques	
	18.4.17	8.30 "	" " " " Arques " Hazebrouck	
	19.4.17	8.15 "	" " " " Hazebrouck " Scherpenberg	
	30.4.17	4.30 pm	" " " " Scherpenberg " Poperinghe	
			" " " " Scherpenberg " Berthen	
	18.4.17	8.15 am	N° 4 Section (58th Inf Bde Signals) " " " Berthen	
	19.4.17	6.0 "	" " " " Berthen " Poperinghe	
	29.4.17	1.30 pm	" " " " Poperinghe " The Ramparts Ypres.	
	30.4.17	12 Noon	" " " "	

E.R.Grove Major R.E.
Commanding 16th Div. Signal Coy. R.E.

WAR DIARY
or
INTELLIGENCE SUMMARY.
(Erase heading not required.)

Army Form C. 2118.

Instructions regarding War Diaries and Intelligence Summaries are contained in F. S. Regs., Part II. and the Staff Manual respectively. Title pages will be prepared in manuscript.

Place	Date	Hour	Summary of Events and Information	Remarks and references to Appendices
In the Field	2.5.17	9.0 am	Coy moved from Westoutre to Busseboom. Office opened there at 10.0 a.m.	
	12.5.17	6.0 "	" " " Busseboom - Westoutre " " 10.0 a.m.	
	14.5.17		Major G.R. Grange R.E. granted Special leave to U.K. from 14/5/17 to 21/5/17	
	20.5.17		II Lieut A Rose R.E. (58th Bde Signals) evacuated to F.d Ambulance (accident)	
	29.5.17		Lieut E Parry joined Unit from Second Army for Temporary duty with 58th Bde Sigs.	
	1.5.17	5:20 pm	No 2 Section (56th Inf Bde Signals) moved from La Clytte to Scherpenberg	
	2.5.17	10.30 am	" " (" " ") " " Scherpenberg - Poperinghe	
	4.5.17	1:30 pm	" " (" " ") " " Poperinghe - La Clytte	
	20.5.17	5:30 pm	" " (" " ") " " La Clytte - Scherpenberg	
	25.5.17	2.0 pm	" " (" " ") " " Scherpenberg - Westoutre (Hurst Park)	
	29.5.17	5:30 pm	" " (" " ") " " Westoutre - La Clytte	
	2.5.17	10:30 am	No 3 Section (59th Inf Bde Signals) " " Poperinghe - Ypres (Rly Dugouts)	
	10.5.17	6.0 pm	" " (" " ") " " Ypres - Poperinghe	
	11.5.17	1:30 pm	" " (" " ") " " Poperinghe - Scherpenberg	
	20.5.17	5.0 pm	" " (" " ") " " Scherpenberg - La Clytte	
	24.5.17	2.0 pm	" " (" " ") " " La Clytte - Westoutre (Hurst Park)	
	12.5.17	10.0 pm	No 4 Section (58th Inf Bde Signals) " " The Ramparts Ypres - Poperinghe	
	13.5.17	3.30 "	" " (" " ") " " Poperinghe - Berthen	
	15.5.17	5.0 am	" " (" " ") " " Berthen - Eblinghem	
	16.5.17	8.20 "	" " (" " ") " " Eblinghem - Arques	
	17.5.17	7.30 "	" " (" " ") " " Arques - Recques (Cocove Chateau)	
	25.5.17	7.30 "	" " (" " ") " " Recques - Scherpenberg. Bivouac from Watton to Bailleul	

E.R. Grange Major R.E.

WAR DIARY
or
INTELLIGENCE SUMMARY.

(Erase heading not required.)

Army Form C. 2118.

Instructions regarding War Diaries and Intelligence Summaries are contained in F. S. Regs., Part II. and the Staff Manual respectively. Title pages will be prepared in manuscript.

19 D Signals Vol 2 4

Place	Date	Hour	Summary of Events and Information	Remarks and references to Appendices
In the Field	1.6.17	9.0 am	Coy moved from Westoutre to Scherpenberg. Office opened at 10.0am	
	2.0.6.17	9.0 "	" " Scherpenberg " St Jans Capell, " " 10.0 "	
	6.6.17	5.0 pm	No 2 Section (56th Inf Bde Signals) moved from La Clytte to Dugouts Bois Carré.	
	8.6.17	8.0 "	" " " " " " Dugouts Bois Carré " Grand Bois	
	15.6.17	8.0 "	" " " " " " Grand Bois " Fairy House	
	18.6.17	2.0 "	" " " " " " Fairy House " Kemmel Hill	
	6.6.17	1.0 "	No 3 Section (57th Inf Bde Signals) " " Hurst Park, Westoutre " Bois Carré B.S.C.	
	7.6.17	3.30 "	" " " " " " Bois Carré B.S.C. " Grand Bois	
	9.6.17	5.0 "	" " " " " " Grand Bois " Bois Carré	
	10.6.17	8.0 "	" " " " " " Bois Carré " La Clytte	
	13.6.17	2.0 "	" " " " " " La Clytte " Fairy House	
	15.6.17	2.0 "	" " " " " " Fairy House " Grand Bois	
	19.6.17	8.0 "	" " " " " " Grand Bois " Locre	
	20.6.17	2.30 "	" " " " " " Locre " Scherpenberg	
	6.6.17	1.30 "	No 4 Section (58th Inf Bde Signals) " " Dugouts X Roads Vierstraat " Bois Carré	
	10.6.17	5.0 "	" " " " " " Bois Carré " Fairy House	
	19.6.17	2.0 am	" " " " " " Fairy House " Camp 54 Div nr Bailleul	
	19.6.17	5.40 pm	" " " " " "	
	16.6.17		Capt H.Carey Thomas RE on leave to UK 16.6.17 to 26.6.17 — 10 days	
	22.6.17		Capt V.R.L. Hay went on Special leave 22.6.17 to 28.6.17 — 6 days	
			" Lieut F.Burnett RE on leave to UK 21.6.17 to 1.7.17 — 10 days	
	23.6.17		" Lieut W.A.Mabison R.E. " " " 23.6.17 to 3.7.17 — 10 "	
	26.6.17		" T.S.E.Perry R.W.F. " " " 20.6.17 to 30.6.17 = 10 "	

E.R.Grange Major R.E.
Commanding 19th Div Signal Coy R.E.

WAR DIARY
or
INTELLIGENCE SUMMARY.
(Erase heading not required.)

Army Form C. 2118.

19 Div. Signal Coy. R.E.

Place	Date	Hour	Summary of Events and Information	Remarks referring to Appendices
In the Field	3.7.17	9.0 am	Company moved from St Jans Cappel to Scherpenberg Office opened at 9.0 am by advance party	
	1.7.17	8.0 am	No 2 Section (56th Inf Bde Signals) moved from Kemmel Hill to Locre	
	19.7.17	2.0 pm	" " " " Locre " Dammstrasse	
	23.7.17	7.0 "	" " " " Dammstrasse " Fairy House	
	24.7.17	2.0 "	" " " " Fairy House " Dammstrasse	
	1.7.17	2.0 pm	No 3 Section (57th Inf Bde Signals) " MontVidaque " SP12	
	2.7.17	2.0 "	" " " " Fairy House " Fairy House	
	12.7.17	9.0 "	" " " " SP12 " Dammstrasse	
	22.7.17	2.0 "	" " " " Fairy House " Fairy House	
	29.7.17	7.0 "	" " " " Dammstrasse " SP12	
	31.7.17	8.0 "	" " " " Fairy House " Fairy House	
	2.7.17	6.30 pm	No 4 Section (58th Inf Bde Signals) " S.A.A.22 " Dammstrasse	
	11.7.17	9.45 "	" " " " Fairy House " Locre	
	19.7.17	9.30 "	" " " " Dammstrasse " SP12	
	29.7.17	5.0 "	" " " " Locre " Parver Farm	
	30.7.17	6.0 "	" " " " SP12 "	
	4.7.17		Capt H.Carey Thomas left Unit to join 6 Div Signal Coy.	
	22.7.17		Lieut R.R.Rawson R.E. joined Unit for duty (vice Capt H.Carey Thomas) from 9th Div Signal Coy.	
	21.7.17		Lieut F.N.Howes R.E. granted leave to UK 21.7.17 to 31.7.17 = 10 days	

C.R.Grange Major R.E.
Comd 19 Div Signal Coy RE

WAR DIARY
or
INTELLIGENCE SUMMARY.
(Erase heading not required.)

Army Form C. 2118.

19 D Signal
Vol 26

Place	Date	Hour	Summary of Events and Information	Remarks and references to Appendices
In the Field	8/8/17	9.0 a.m	Coy moved from Scherpenberg to St Jans Cappel. Office opened at 10.0 am	
	11/8/17	8.0 "	" St Jans Cappel to Lumbres. " " 12.0 noon by advance party	
	28/8/17	8.0 "	" Lumbres " St Jans Cappel. " " 12.0 " " "	
			at Lumbres Closed at Noon on 29" Office Staff proceeding by Motor Lorry afterwards and office	
	3/8/17	6.30 pm	No 2 Section (56" Inf Bde Signals) moved from Jan Shwasse to Locre	
	6/8/17	"	" " " " " " " MtKokereele	
	10/8/17	"	" " " " " " " Colembert	
	23/8/17	"	" " " " " " " Nielles-Lez-Bleguin	
	28/8/17	"	" " " " " " " Mt Noir	
			" " " " " " SP12	
			" " " " " " Fairy House Locre	
	1/9/17	6.30 pm	No 3 Section (57 Inf Bde Signals) " " " Fairy House	
	2/9/17	2.0 "	" " " " " Jamshwasse	
	7/9/17	7.30 "	" " " " " Fairy House	
	8/9/17	6.0 "	" " " " " Mt Noir	
	10/9/17	6.15 "	" " " " " Wizernes (by train from Gaillee)	
	11/9/17	7.30 am	" " " " " Nielles-lez-Bleguin	
	21/9/17	9.30 "	" " " " " Columbert	
	23/9/17	7.0 "	" " " " " Le Meppe	
	29/9/17	9.0 "	" " " " " 1Mle Sd Flerve.	
	7/9/17	7.0 pm	No 4 Section (58" Inf Bde Signals) " St B 62 near St Jans Cappel	
	10/9/17	1.30 "	" " " " " Lumbres	
	28/9/17	3.0 "	" " " " " MtKokereele	
	10/9/17	1.0 pm	R.A. H.Q Section Signals " " L'Epinette Farm	
	29/9/17	9.0 am	" " " " " Courte Croix	
	23/9/17	8.0 "	" " " " " Mervis	

Army Form C. 2118.

WAR DIARY
or
INTELLIGENCE SUMMARY.

(Erase heading not required.)

2

Instructions regarding War Diaries and Intelligence
Summaries are contained in F. S. Regs., Part II.
and the Staff Manual respectively. Title pages
will be prepared in manuscript.

Place	Date	Hour	Summary of Events and Information	Remarks and references to Appendices
In the Field	10/8/17	9.0am	87th Bde R.F.A Signal Sub Section moved from Vandamme Farm I 5 X.17.6.6 " Strazeele	
	10/8/17	1.0pm	" " " " " " " " X.17.6.6 " Eqcudescure	
	10/8/17	6.0 "	" " 88th " " " " " Grand Bois " Meuvis	
	11/8/17	9.0am	" " 89th " " " " " Caudescure	

R Rawson Capt/EA. Major R.E.

Commanding 19th Divl Signal Coy. R.E.

WAR DIARY
or
INTELLIGENCE SUMMARY.

(Erase heading not required.)

Army Form C. 2118.

31 Inf Bde 19D Signal 9/17 27

Place	Date	Hour	Summary of Events and Information	Remarks and references to Appendices
In the field.	12.9.17	9.0am	Coy moved from St Jans Cappel to Scherpenberg. Office opened at 10.0am.	
	16.9.17	10.0am	No. 2 Section (56th Bde Signals) moved from Mt Noir to Locre	
	19.9.17	8.30pm	" " " " Locre " Spoil Bank	
	29.9.17	4.0 "	" " " " Spoil Bank " Kemmel	
	6.9.17	9.30am	No 3 " " Courte Croix " Mont Vidaigne	
	11.9.17	2.0pm	" " " " Mont Vidaigne " Spoil Bank	
	14.9.17	12.0pm	" " " " Spoil Bank " Fairy House	
	18.9.17	4.0 "	" " " " Fairy House " Hill 60	
	22.9.17	6.0am	" " " " Hill 60 " Fairy House	
	27.9.17	3.0pm	No 4 " " Fairy House " Lauch Wood	
	10.9.17	9.30am	" " 58° " McKokeveele " Fairy House	
	11.9.17	4.0pm	" " " " Fairy House " Spoil Bank	
	14.9.17	4.0 "	" " " " Spoil Bank " Locre	
	18.9.17	6.0am	" " " " Locre " Hill 60	
	22.9.17	2.0pm	" " " " Hill 60 " Rossignal Camp	
	29.9.17	6.0am	HQ r" " (Div R.A) " Rossignal Camp " Spoil Bank " St Jans Cappel	
	2.9.17	9.0am	" " " " Mervis " St Jans Cappel	
	5.9.17	9.0am	" " " " St Jans Cappel " Scherpenberg	
	6.9.17	9.0am	Sub Sect 67 Bde (R.A. Sigs) " Strazeele " O.2.a.8.0	
	22.9.17	6.0 "	" " 88° " (" ") " O.2.a.8.0 " N16 C 9.4	
	6.9.17	9.0 "	" " " " (" ") " Mervis " Siege Farm N16C29	

II Lieut A. Rose R.E. "wounded in action 19.9.17
" T.S.E. Parry R.W.F " " 20.9.17
Lieut W.A. Nitchison R.E. "Killed " " 20.9.17

WAR DIARY
or
INTELLIGENCE SUMMARY.

Army Form C. 2118.

Place	Date	Hour	Summary of Events and Information	Remarks and references to Appendices
	26.9.17		Lt Lonsdale. W.S. R.E from IX Corps exchanged with Lieut R. Juckes R.E	
	26.9.17		2nd Lieut L.G Maden Joined Unit from IX Corps Sigs Vice Lieut W.A. Mitchison "Killed in action"	
	27.9.17		" " H.R. Iliffe " " " Second Army " T.S.E Parry R.W.F "Wounded in action"	
	29.9.17		2nd Lieut C.F. Curtis " " " IX Corps Cavalry " 2nd " H. Rose R.E " "	

Capt. R.E.
Commanding 19th Div. Signal Coy. R.E.

WAR DIARY
or
INTELLIGENCE SUMMARY.
(Erase heading not required.)

Army Form C. 2118.

19 D Signals Vol 28

Place	Date	Hour	Summary of Events and Information	Remarks and references to Appendices
In the Field	5.10.17		No 2. Section (56th Inf Bde Signals) moved from Rossignal Camp Kemmel to Lock 8	
	14.10.17		" " (" " ") " " " " Tournai Camp	
	19.10.17		" " (" " ") " " " " Rossignal Camp, Kemmel	
	27.10.17		" " (" " ") " " " " Spoil Bank	
	5.10.17	6.0pm	No 3 Section (57th Inf Bde Signals) " " Larch Wood " Rossignal Camp	
	11.10.17	1.0 "	" " (" " ") " " " " Rossignal Camp	
	19.10.17	4.0 "	" " (" " ") " " " " Spoil Bank	
	27.10.17	2.0 "	" " (" " ") " " " " Tournai Camp	
	30.10.17	2.30 "	" " (" " ") " " " " Rossignal Camp	
	5.10.17		No 4 Section (58t Inf Bde Signals) " " " " Spoil Bank	
	11.10.17		" " (" " ") " " " " Rossignal Camp	
	19.10.17		" " (" " ") " " " " Spoil Bank	
	30.10.17		" " (" " ") " " " " Kemmel Chateau	

E.R.Gjanos Major RE
Commanding 19th Div. Signal Coy. R.E.

WAR DIARY
or
INTELLIGENCE SUMMARY

Army Form C. 2118.

19 D Signals
Vol 27

Place	Date	Hour	Summary of Events and Information	Remarks and references to Appendices
In the Field	10.11.17	9.00am	Coy moved from Scherpenberg to St Jans Cappel. Office opened at 10.0am	
	12.11.17	9.0 "	St Jans Cappel to Blaringhem. Office opened at 10.0am	
	4.11.17	2.0pm	No 2 Section (56th Bde Signals) moved from Spoil Bank to Kemmel Chateau	
	8.11.17	9-00am	" " " " (" ") " " Kemmel Chateau to Locre	
	9.11.17	9.00 "	" " " " (" ") " " Locre " Inkerman Camp	
	10.11.17	9.00 "	" " " " (" ") " " Inkerman Camp " Wallon-Cappel	
	4.11.17	Noon	No 3 Section (57th Bde Signals) " " Fairy House Locre " Spoil Bank	
	9.11.17	2.0pm	" " " " (" ") " " Spoil Bank " Kemmel	
	10.11.17	9.00am	" " " " (" ") " " Kemmel " Mervis	
	12.11.17	10.30 "	" " " " (" ") " " Mervis " Pont Asquim (Reniscure)	
	20.11.17	1.0pm	" " " " (" ") " " Pont Asquim " Wardrecques	
	4.11.17	9.00am	No 4 Section (58th Bde Signals) " " Kemmel Chateau " Fairy House	
	8.11.17	9.0am	" " " " (" ") " " Fairy House " Strazeele	
	11.11.17	9.00am	" " " " (" ") " " Strazeele " Ebblinghem	
	20.11.17	10.30am	" " " " (" ") " " Ebblinghem " Le Mt D'Hiver Chateau	

C.V. Grange Major R.E.
Commdg 19th Div Signal Coy R.E.

WAR DIARY or INTELLIGENCE SUMMARY

Army Form C. 2118.

19th Divl Signal Coy

Place	Date	Hour	Summary of Events and Information	Remarks and references to Appendices
In the Field	5.12.17	12.0 noon	Company moved from Blaringham to Arcques Station for Entrainment. Entrained at 4.30pm for Beaumetz Station arriving about 12.30pm. After entrainment marched to Basseux. Officers at Basseux observed at noon by advance party.	
	8.12.17	Noon	Coy moved from Basseux to Achiet-le-Petit	
	9.12.17	9.0 am	" " Achiet-le-Petit to Ervicourt	
	12.12.17	4.0 "	" " Ervicourt to Neuville	
	6.12.17		No 2 Section (5"U" F.S. 3rd Signals) moved from Wallon Cappel to Bailleulmont	
	8.12.17		" " Bailleulmont " Courcelles-les-Comptes	
	9.12.17		" " Courcelles-les-Comptes " Mamancourt	
	11.12.17		" " Mamancourt " Ribecourt Section	
	28.12.17		" " Ribecourt Section " Ruyalcourt	
	9.12.17	8.0 am	No 3 Section (57th Inf Bde Signals) " Waydrecques " Pomiers	
	8.12.17	11.0 am	" " Pomiers " Ervicourt	
	9.12.17	12.30 pm	" " Ervicourt " Bde Support	
	10.12.17	5.0 "	" " Bde Support " Ribecourt	
	15.12.17	6.30 "	" " Ribecourt " Bde Support (Jehaud Ribecourt)	
	19.12.17	3.0 pm	" " Bde Support " Ribecourt	
	23.12.17	4.0 "	" " Ribecourt " Bde Support	
	7.12.17	11.0 am	No 4 Section (58th Inf Bde Signals) " Royalcourt " Ridge Redoubt	
	8.12.17	9.0 am	" " Mont D'Hiver " Blaireville	
	9.12.17	9.0 "	" " Blaireville " Gomiecourt	
	11.12.17	7.0 "	" " Gomiecourt " Ervicourt	
	12.12.17	6.0 "	" " Ervicourt " Bde Support behind Ribecourt	
	13.12.17	4.0 pm	" " Bde Support " Bde H.Qrs in line	
	15.12.17	5.0 "	" " Bde H.Qrs " Ruyalcourt	
	28.12.17	2.0 "	" " Ruyalcourt " Ribecourt	

Army Form C. 2118.

WAR DIARY
or
INTELLIGENCE SUMMARY.
(Erase heading not required.)

Instructions regarding War Diaries and Intelligence Summaries are contained in F. S. Regs., Part II. and the Staff Manual respectively. Title pages will be prepared in manuscript.

Place	Date	Hour	Summary of Events and Information	Remarks and references to Appendices
In the Field	13.11.17		H.Q. in Section (R.A Signals) moved from St Jans Cappel to Neuville	
	19.11.17		86° Bde. R.F.A Signal Sub Section " Locre 7. to La Clytte	
	22.12.17		La Clytte " Oudendom	
	30.11.17		Oudendom and entrained at Bailleul for Bapaume	
	31.11.17		Bapaume to Rocquigny	

E.P. George Major R.E.
Superintending 19th Div. Signal Coy. R.E.

WAR DIARY
or
INTELLIGENCE SUMMARY.
(Erase heading not required.)

Army Form C. 2118.

Place	Date	Hour	Summary of Events and Information	Remarks and references to Appendices
In the field	3.1.18	2.0 pm	No. 2 Section (56th Inf Bde Signals) moved from Ruyalcourt to Beaucamp Sector	
	12.1.18	3.30 "	" " " " " Beaucamp Sector " Ruyalcourt	
	18.1.18	2.0 "	" " " " " Ruyalcourt " Left Sector L32.A2.2	
	7.1.18	2.30 pm	No. 3 Section (57th Inf Bde Signals) " Sunken Road " Ruyalcourt	
	12.1.18	2.15 "	" " " " " Ruyalcourt " Beaucamp	
	24.1.18	3.30 "	" " " " " Beaucamp " Ruyalcourt	
	4.1.18	6.0 "	No. 4 Section (58th Inf Bde Signals) " Ritecourt " Ruyalcourt	
	5.1.18	2.0 "	" " " " " Ruyalcourt " Left Sector L32a22	
	18.1.18	4.0 "	" " " " " Left Sector L32A122 " Ruyalcourt	
	22.1.18	1.30 "	" " " " " Ruyalcourt " Beaucamp	
	11.1.18	2.0 "	87 Bde R.F.F. Sub Section Signals " L.31 d Central " Neuville	
	23.1.18	1.30 "	" " " " Neuville " Q.m.a.2.6	
	3.1.18	10.00 am	88th Bde " " " Rocquigny " K.36.a.6.0	
	25.1.18		Major G.R. Grange, R.E., DSO, M.C. granted leave to UK 25.1.18 to 15.2.18.	

R. Mawson — Capt R E
Commanding 29th Div. Signal Coy. R.E.

ON HIS MAJESTY'S SERVICE.

Secret.
19th Divisional Signal Coy. R.E.
War Diary for
January 1915

B.

WAR DIARY or INTELLIGENCE SUMMARY

Army Form C. 2118

(Erase heading not required.)

19th D Signals Vol 3

February 1918.

Place	Date	Hour	Summary of Events and Information	Remarks and references to Appendices
Field	15.2.18	9·0am	Coy moved from Neuville to Haplincourt. Office opened at 10.0am.	
	2.2.18	4·30pm	Nº 2 Section (56th Bde Signals) moved from Left Sector Beaucamp to Ytres	
	8.2.18	2·30 "	" " " " Ytres " Right Sector Beaucamp	
	14.2.18	6·0 "	" " " " Right Sector Beaucamp " Barastre	
	23.2.18	8·0 "	" " " " Barastre " Bouzencourt	
	2.2.18	2·30pm	Nº 3 " " " " Rocquelcourt " Hindenburg Line Trescault	
	13.2.18	11·0 "	" " " " Hindenburg Line " Beaulencourt	
	8.2.18	4·30pm	Nº 4 " " " " Beaucamp " Ytres	
	15.2.18	9·0am	" " " " Ytres " Rocquigny	
	23.2.18	2·0pm	" " " " Rocquigny " O.S.C.8.8.	
	15.2.18	9·0am	H.Q. R.A. Sigs " " Neuville " Haplincourt	
	"	4·30pm	87th Bde R.F.A Sub Sections " " Q.12.a.26 " Neuville	

C.R.Grange Major R.E
Commandg 19th Div. Signal Coy.

WAR DIARY
or
INTELLIGENCE SUMMARY

Army Form C. 2118

19th Divl Signals

March 1918   Vol 3

(Erase heading not required.)

Instructions regarding War Diaries and Intelligence Summaries are contained in F.S. Regs., Part II. and the Staff Manual respectively. Title Pages will be prepared in manuscript.

Place	Date	Hour	Summary of Events and Information	Remarks and references to Appendices
Field	1.3.18	10.0 a	Company moved to Hablincourt	
	22.3.18	—	" " " Barancourt	
	22.3.18	8.30p	" " " Greuillers	
	24.3.18	3.30p	" " " Achiet le Petit	
	25.3.18	10.30 am	" " " Puisieux	
	25.3.18	1.30p	" " " Colin Camps	
	25.3.18	6.0p	" " " Longuevillers	
	26.3.18	9.0 a	" " " Pommier	
	26.3.18	5.0 p	" " " La Bouchie	(Kept Ohms at Y.Y.R until 9.30pm) 23 March
	29.3.18	8.30 am	" " Entrained at Doullens	
	29.3.18	4.30 pm	" " Detrained at Strazeele	
	29.3.18	9.0	" " moved to Dramoutre	
	30.3.19		At Dramoutre	
	30.3.19		"	

R.R.Rawson Capt. R.E.
Commanding 19th Divl. Signal Coy. R.E.

19th Divisional Engineers

19th DIVISIONAL SIGNAL COMPANY R. E.

APRIL 1918.

Army Form C. 2118

WAR DIARY
or
INTELLIGENCE SUMMARY
(Erase heading not required.)

19th Divisional Signal Company April 1918 Vol 36

Instructions regarding War Diaries and Intelligence Summaries are contained in F.S. Regs., Part II. and the Staff Manual respectively. Title Pages will be prepared in manuscript.

Place	Date	Hour	Summary of Events and Information	Remarks and references to Appendices
Field	1.4.18		At Dranoutre.	
	2.4.18	10.0 am	Company moved from Dranoutre to Westhof Farm.	
	10.4.18	11.0 pm	Westhof Farm - Dranoutre	
	12.4.18	8.0 am	Dranoutre - Mont Noir	
	15.4.18	Midnt	Mont Noir - Westoutre	
	17.4.18	3.0 am	Westoutre - Boeschepe Area (27 Divn)	
	19.4.18	10.0 am	Boeschepe - Abeele	
	21.4.18	11.30 am	Abeele - Proven Q Staff remained at Watou (K18.A9.9)	27.4.18
	27.4.18	10.0 am	Proven - Watou (K18.A9.9)	
	28.4.18		At Watou (K18.A9.9)	
	29.4.18		"	
	30.4.18		"	

RMann Captain RE
Commanding 19th Div. Signal Coy. R.E.

Army Form C. 2118.

WAR DIARY
or
INTELLIGENCE SUMMARY.
(Erase heading not required.)

19th Signals

May 1918 Vol 35

Place	Date	Hour	Summary of Events and Information	Remarks and references to Appendices
Field	1/5/18	—	At Wattau (K18 A9.9)	
	13/5/18	11.0 am	Company moved from Wattau (K18 A9.9) to Bambecque - Rexpoede	
	16/5/18	1.0 am	" Bambecque - Rexpoede	
	—	3.30 am	Entrained at Rexpoede.	
	18/5/18	5.0 am	De-trained. Chalons.	
	18/5/18	9.5 am	arrived St. Germain	
	28/5/18	11.0 am	Company left St Germain for new area.	
	28/5/18	10.0 pm	Two office reliefs entrained " "	
	29/5/18	4.0 am	Office opened at Chaumuzy.	
	30/5/18	9.30 pm	Moved from Chaumuzy to Pourcy.	
	31/5/18	—	At Pourcy.	

P. Mann Capt. R.E.
Commanding 19th Div. Signal Coy. R.E.

WAR DIARY or **INTELLIGENCE SUMMARY**
(Erase heading not required.)

19 D Signals
June 1918
96 — 36

Army Form C. 2118.

Place	Date	Hour	Summary of Events and Information	Remarks and references to Appendices
	1.6.18	1.0 am	Divisional H.Q. at POURCY and Advanced DHQ CHAUMUZY.	
	1.6.18	3.0 pm	Signal Office transferred to cellar, owing to shell fire	
	1.6.18	10.45 am	DHQ closed at POURCY and opened same town on track ½ kilo NE of church in NANTEUIL.	
	1.6.18	10.45 am	ASP to CUIS.	
	2.6.18		P.R. moved to BULLIN.	
	3.6.18	11.30 am	Communications as per diagram attached (Appendix 1)	
	6.6.18	10.0	P.R. and Brigade Hqrs move from BULLIN to BOIS DE COURTON.	
	11.6.18	1.0	Divisional communications as per diagram attached (Appendix 2)	
	13.6.18	11.0	Communications of Infantry Bdes in the line as per diagram attached (Appendix 3)	
	26.6.18	5.30	Relief of Divn by 8th Italian Divn. Relief complete 12 noon	
			DHQ open at CUIS	
	21.6.18	12.0 noon	DHQ closed CUIS and reopened MONTGIVRAUX CHATEAU	
	30.6.18	10.0 pm	Report centre opened IX Corps HQ. FERE CHAMPENOISE.	
		midnight	DHQ closed MONTGIVRAUX CHATEAU.	

Commanding 19th Div. Signal Coy. R.E.

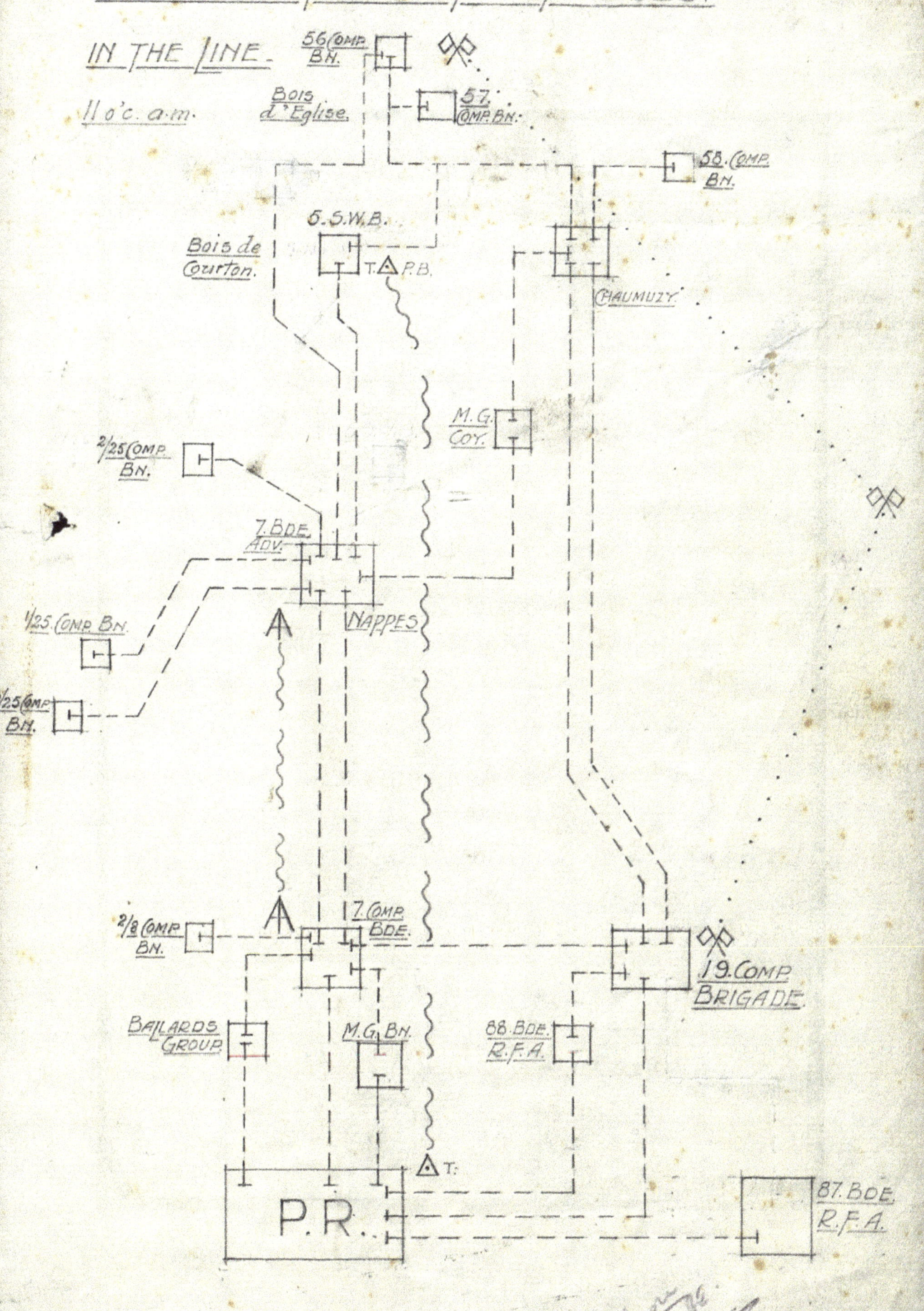

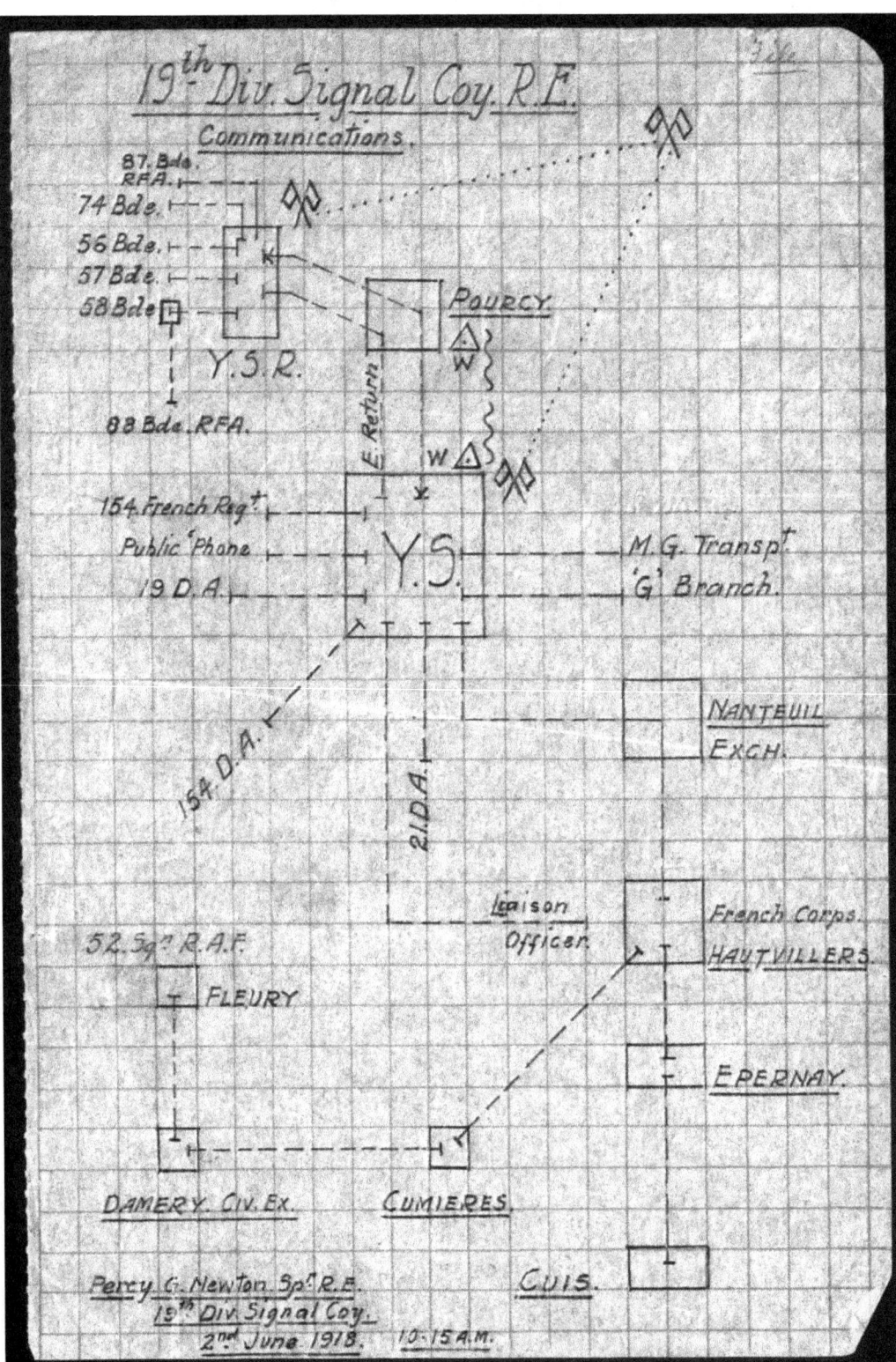

19 Div. Signal Coy. R.E.
Communications.

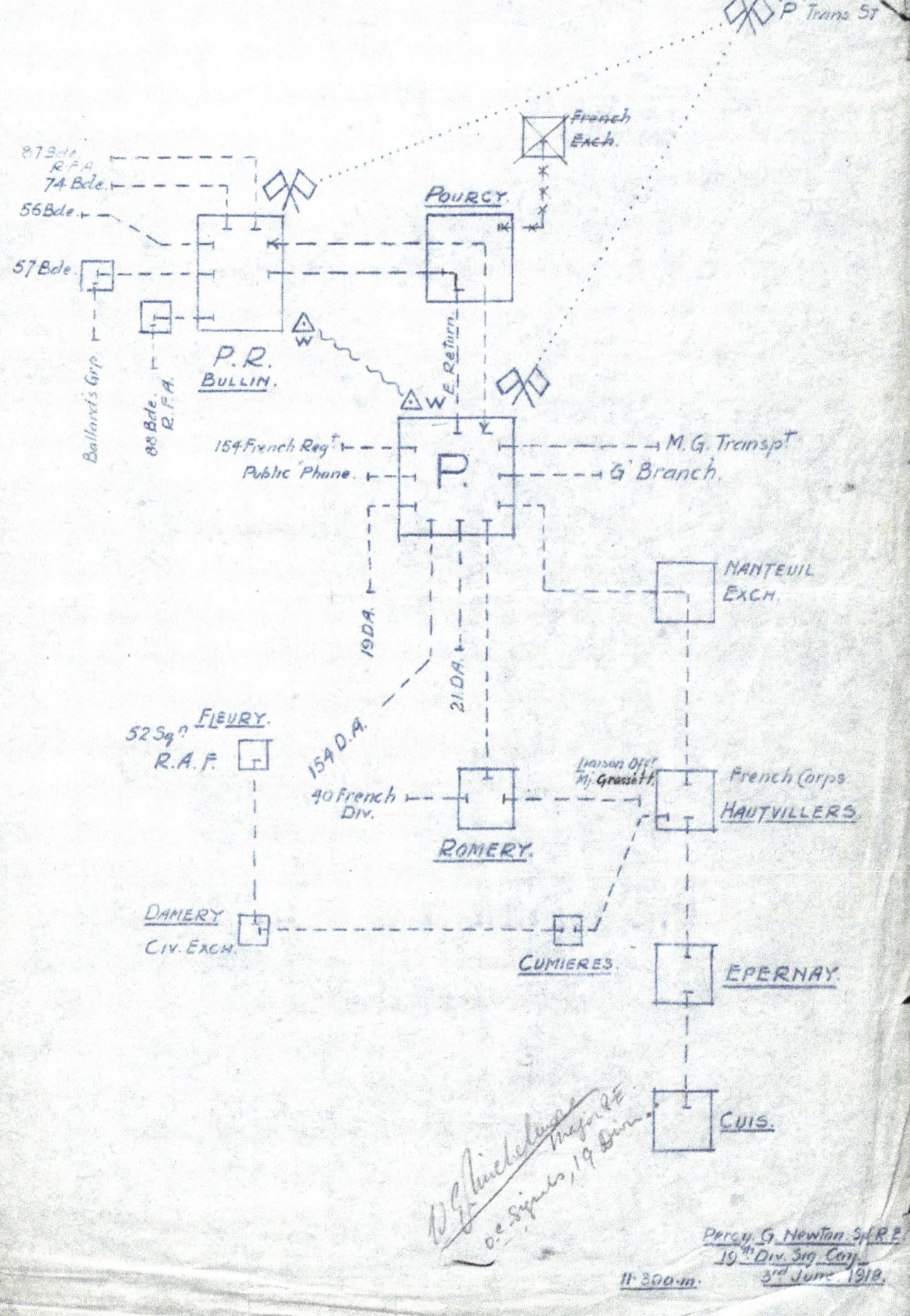

Percy G. Newton, S/LtRE
19th Div. Sig. Coy.
3rd June 1918.

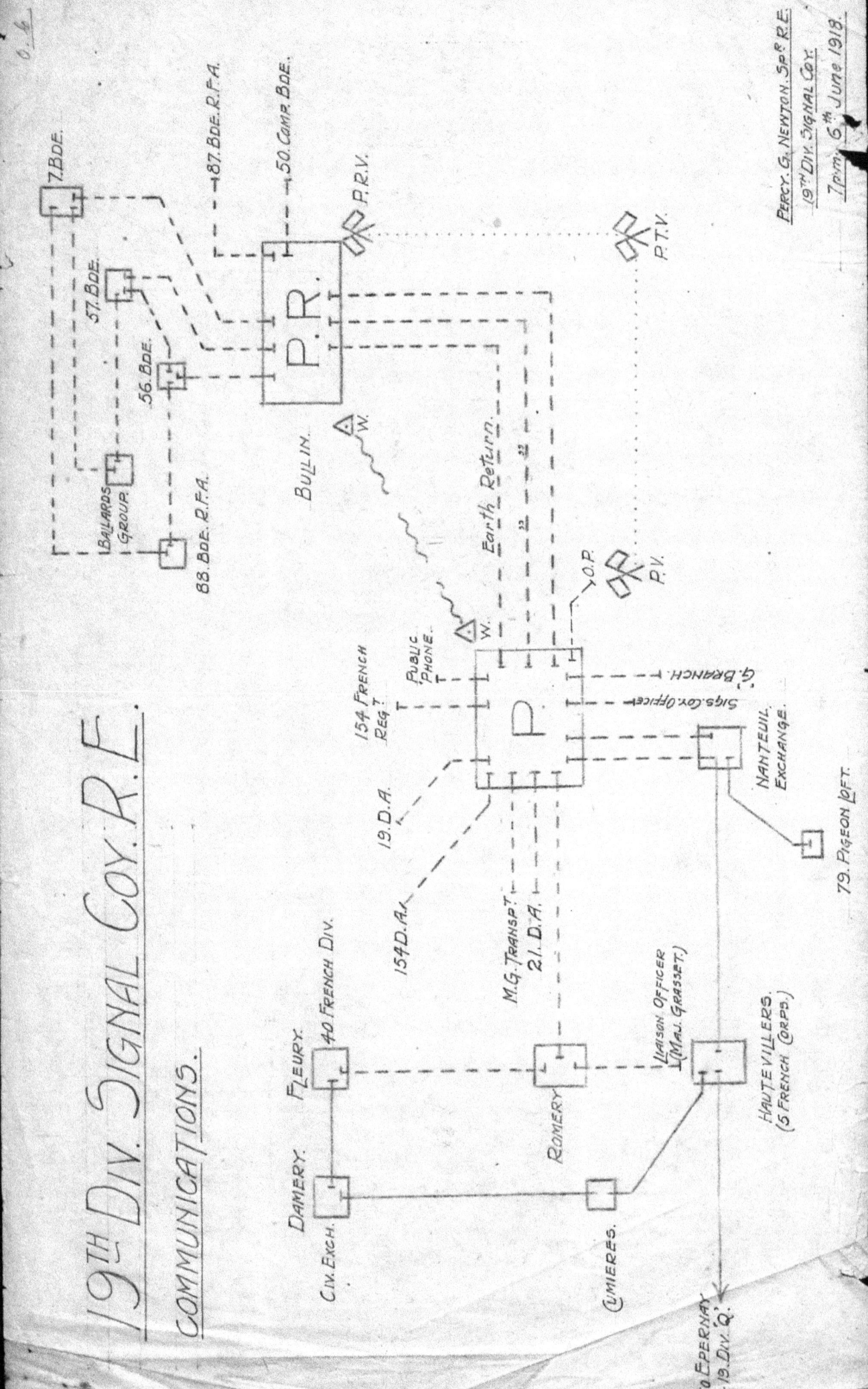

WAR DIARY
or
INTELLIGENCE SUMMARY.

(Erase heading not required.)

19 D Signals
July 1918
Vol 37

Place	Date	Hour	Summary of Events and Information	Remarks and references to Appendices
	1.7.18	10.0 am	DHQ Report Centre IX Corps closed. Company entrained at SOMMESOUS	
	2.7.18	8.#5 pm	Company arrived at ANVIN and proceeded by march route to HERVARRE CHATEAU	
	3.7.18	12.0 noon	DHQ opened HERVARRE CHATEAU.	
	11.7.18	9.30 am	Advance Party (office relief Linemen) proceeded to BOMY.	
	12.7.18	8.30 am	Company proceeded by march route from HERVARRE to BOMY	
	12.7.18	12.0 noon	DHQ opened 12.0 noon at BOMY.	
	31.7.18			

W. G. Nicholson
Major RE
Commanding 19th Div. Signal Coy. R.E.

19 D Signal Army Form C. 2118.

6
9/256

WAR DIARY
INTELLIGENCE SUMMARY.

August 1918.   Vol 38

Place	Date	Hour	Summary of Events and Information	Remarks and references to Appendices
Field	1.8.18	—	At BOMY.	
"	6.8.18	3.30p	Advanced party (1 Office Relief and linemen) proceeded to LA'BEUVRIERE	
"	6.8.18	1.30p	Company proceeded by march route to LA'BEUVRIERE	
"	7.8.18	10.0 a	Divl Headqrs closed BOMY and opened LA'BEUVRIERE.	
"	31.8.18	—	At LA'BEUVRIERE.	

Signature
Major R.E.
Commanding 19th Divl. Signal Coy. R.E.

19 D Signal, Army Form C. 2118.

September 1918.

WAR DIARY
or
INTELLIGENCE SUMMARY.
(Erase heading not required.)

Place	Date	Hour	Summary of Events and Information	Remarks and references to Appendices
Field	1.9.18		At LABEUVRIERE.	
	2.9.18	1030	Advanced Report Centre opened at H.S.	
	4.9.18	1600	Advanced Report Centre moved from H.S. to R.35.b.4.1	
	5.9.18	0830	Company transport moved from LABEUVRIERE by march route to W.30.a.7.8	
	5.9.18	1000	Advanced party (Signal Office Relief) proceeded to W.30.a.7.8	
	6.9.18	1200	DHQ closed LABEUVRIERE, and opened W.30.a.7.8 same hour.	
	12.9.18	1600	Advanced Report Centre moved from R.35.b.4.1 to R.34.d.7.8	
	30.9.18		At W.30.a.7.8.	

Commanding 19th Div. Signal Coy, R.E.

19 D Signal
19
146
Army Form C. 2118.

WAR DIARY
INTELLIGENCE SUMMARY
October 1918.

Place	Date	Hour	Summary of Events and Information	Remarks and references to Appendices
Field	1.10.18		At LAWESIDE W30a78.	
	3.10.18	0930	DHQ closed W30a78 and opened same hour at AUCHEL. Company transport proceeded by march route 0800 hours.	
	4.10.18	0200	Company transport left AUCHEL, and proceeded by march route for HENU, bivouacing night 4/5th in neighbourhood of MANIN.	
	4.10.18	0930	DHQ closed AUCHEL arrives HENU 1600	
	5.10.18	0800	Signal Office opened at HENU.	
	6.10.18	0800	Company transport left HENU for GRAINCOURT bivouacing night 6/7 in neighbourhood of FREMICOURT. Advance Office Relief and linemen left HQ at 0930.	
	7.10.18	11.35	DHQ closes HENU opens at GRAINCOURT. 1400 hours.	
	9.10.18	17.15	DHQ closes GRAINCOURT opened at NOYELLES. same hour.	
	13.10.18	1400	DHQ closes NOYELLES opened CAMBRAI A23b 1500.	
	18.10.18	1000	DHQ closes A23b. opened AVESNES-LEZ-AUBERT same hour.	
	19.10.18	1715	Advanced Report Centre established at ST AUBERT.	
	20.10.18	1330	Rear Signal Office closes AVESNES.	
	24.10.18	1100	DHQ closes ST-AUBERT. opens AVESNES	
	31.10.18		at AVESNES-LEZ-AUBERT.	

A.J. Nicholson
Major
Commanding 19th Div. Signal Coy. R.E.